WOMEN OF THE BIBLE

JEAN E. SYSWERDA
BESTSELLING AUTHOR

ZONDERVAN®

ZONDERVAN

Women of the Bible: 52 Bible Studies for Individuals and Groups
Copyright © 1999, 2002 by Ann Spangler and Jean Syswerda

An abridgment of *Women of the Bible*
Copyright © 1999 by Ann Spangler and Jean Syswerda

Requests for information should be addressed to:
Zondervan, 3900 *Sparks Dr. SE, Grand Rapids, Michigan* 49546

ISBN 978-0-310-09670-2

Published in association with Wolgemuth and Associates, Inc., 8600 Crestgate Circle, Orlando, FL 32819.

Interior design: Susan Ambs

First printing February 2010 / Printed in the United States of America

TO MY DAUGHTERS,
HOLLY AND SHELLY
You have shown me the beauty of young women of God

CONTENTS

ALPHABETICAL INDEX OF WOMEN

INTRODUCTION

Look at the women in Scripture and you will see more than just some women who lived thousands of years ago. You'll see yourself. As you study their stories and immerse yourself in their lives, you'll see more and more places where your life intersects with theirs.

Women of the Bible: 52 Bible Studies for Individuals and Groups presents 52 women of Scripture. Beginning with a short description of the woman, then continuing with her story from Scripture and something about her life and times, each woman's story ends with a study that asks the hard questions. How does her life mirror yours? What did she learn or experience that you as a God-follower yet need to learn or experience? What event or relationship or crisis in her life reveals something about your life? Even more than that, each study will help you discover how God is revealing himself to you through that woman's story. We encourage you as an individual or group not to pass over the questions that are hard or make you uncomfortable. The women of God's Word have much to offer you, but only if you face them openly and honestly.

Charts that will provide depth and meaning to your reflections accompany a number of the studies. From a chart of the Herod family (see page 238) to a chart of the women in Jesus' life (see page 235) to a comprehensive listing of all the women in the Bible (see page 225), *Women of the Bible: 52 Bible Studies for Individuals and Groups* will furnish the background information that makes a Bible study not just titillating but stimulating as well.

Women of the Bible: 52 Bible Studies for Individuals and Groups is an abridgment of a much larger work, the best-selling book *Women of the Bible*, coauthored by Jean Syswerda and Ann Spangler. This study edition of that book is designed specifically so individuals and groups can delve more deeply into the lives of these biblical women. Without hesitation or compromise, *Women of the Bible: 52 Bible Studies for Individuals and Groups* will lead you on a journey of discovery ... discovering things about the women of the Bible, about your God, and about yourself.

In addition to the debt I owe to Ann for her work on the original book, Ann and I both owe a special debt of gratitude to our editors, Sandy Vander Zicht, for her insight, encouragement, and advocacy, Rachel Boers, for her skilled and painstaking work on the manuscript of the original book, and Lori VandenBosch and Dirk Buursma, for their diligent attention to the details of this study edition. We are also grateful to our agent, Robert Wolgemuth, and to Sue Brower and her creative marketing team, for catching the vision for this book. Thanks also goes to Leanne Van Dyk, for her insightful theological review and comments. Few books succeed without champions, and we are grateful that these are some of ours.

It is my hope and prayer that *Women of the Bible: 52 Bible Studies for Individuals and Groups* will lead you as an individual or group into a deeper love for God's Word and its truth in your life. May the example set by these women so many years ago shine the light of God's presence on the pathway of your life today.

—Jean Syswerda, April 2002

1

EVE

Her Name Means "Life-giving"
or "Mother of All Who Have Life"

HER CHARACTER: She came into the world perfectly at peace with her God and with her husband, the only other person on the planet. She lived in Paradise, possessing every pleasure imaginable. She never knew the meaning of embarrassment, misunderstanding, hurt, estrangement, envy, bitterness, grief, or guilt until she listened to her enemy and began to doubt God.

KEY SCRIPTURES: Genesis 1:26–31; Genesis 2–4

The man gave names to all the livestock, the birds of the air and all the beasts of the field.

But for Adam no suitable helper was found. So the LORD God caused the man to fall into a deep sleep; and while he was sleeping, he took one of the man's ribs and closed up the place with flesh. Then the LORD God made a woman from the rib he had taken out of the man, and he brought her to the man.

The man said,

"This is now bone of my bones
and flesh of my flesh;
she shall be called 'woman,'
for she was taken out of man."

For this reason a man will leave his father and mother and be united to his wife, and they will become one flesh.

The man and his wife were both naked, and they felt no shame.

Now the serpent was more crafty than any of the wild animals the LORD God had made. He said to the woman, "Did God really say, 'You must not eat from any tree in the garden'?"

The woman said to the serpent, "We may eat fruit from the trees in the garden, but God did say, 'You must not eat fruit from the tree that is in the middle of the garden, and you must not touch it, or you will die.'"

Notes

"You will not surely die," the serpent said to the woman. "For God knows that when you eat of it your eyes will be opened, and you will be like God, knowing good and evil."

When the woman saw that the fruit of the tree was good for food and pleasing to the eye, and also desirable for gaining wisdom, she took some and ate it. She also gave some to her husband, who was with her, and he ate it. Then the eyes of both of them were opened, and they realized they were naked; so they sewed fig leaves together and made coverings for themselves.

. . . So the LORD God said to the serpent, "Because you have done this,

"Cursed are you above all the livestock
  and all the wild animals!
You will crawl on your belly
  and you will eat dust
  all the days of your life."

GENESIS 2:20–3:7, 14

Eve's Life and Times

Childbirth

Eve was the first woman to conceive a child, the first to harbor a fertilized egg in her womb. Did she understand the miracle taking place within her as her belly swelled and her child began to move? Did she know the wonder of love for a child yet unborn? The Bible doesn't give us those answers. But it does tell us that Eve recognized that life was in God's control. At Cain's birth she exclaimed, "With the help of the Lord, I have brought forth a man" (Genesis 4:1).

God's judgment on Eve—"with pain you will give birth to children"—was no doubt exactly what Eve experienced in birthing this first child. It's the process we appropriately term labor. Eve likely bore the pain and went through the entire birth with only Adam's help.

Later, Hebrew women had the help of experienced midwives, who knew remedies for common delivery difficulties. Midwives' responsibilities after the birth included cutting the umbilical cord, washing the newborn, rubbing it with salt for cleansing, and then wrapping it in swaddling cloths.

The birth stool referred to in Exodus 1:16 was probably a low stool on which the mother-to-be squatted, allowing the force of gravity to aid in the birth process. The midwife and possibly other close relatives held the mother's hands to give comfort as well as stability as the mother bore down.

Our Life and Times

Women throughout the centuries have borne the results of Eve's sin. Their pain in childbearing unites them in a common bond of an experience shared. The experience is an unusual combination of the earthy and at the same time the unearthly. The pains, the panting, the mess and disorder connected with the birth of a child are of the earth, of Eve herself. But what is brought forth, and the bond between the mother and the child of this experience, is unearthly, something only the Creator of life could forge.

Eve's Legacy in Scripture

Read Genesis 2:21–25.

1. Describe Adam's situation (2:18, 20). In this paradise, what need did he have that only a woman could fulfill?

2. What does being "one flesh" (2:24) in a marriage mean, both physically and spiritually?

3. Think of a couple who truly seems to be "one flesh." What is their relationship like?

Read Genesis 3:1–13.

4. Genesis 3:1–5 is one of the saddest passages in Scripture, but also the one that sets the stage for all that is to come. How easily do you think the serpent deceived Eve? Do you think she ate of the fruit the first time he approached her, or did he wear her down over a period of time?

5. Why did Eve eat the fruit (3:6)?

6. Eve is rationalizing her sin here. Even though she knew it was wrong, she came up with three reasons for eating from the tree. What sorts of reasons do you come up with to rationalize your sin?

7. Adam and Eve produce a classic scene of passing the blame: Adam blames Eve; Eve blames the serpent (3:12–13). Is any one of the three participants any more or less to blame? What do the curses God pronounces on each tell you about who is "at fault" (3:14–19)?

Read Genesis 3:20–24.

8. What is the first thing God does for Adam and Eve after he declares what their punishment will be?

9. What does God's act tell you about him? What do you think he is willing to do for you after you have sinned and repented?

Read Genesis 4:1–2.

10. Whom does Eve acknowledge as the source of life (4:1)?

11. Eve now has two sons (4:2). Cain's name is Hebrew for "brought forth," while Abel's name means "breath" or "temporary" or "meaningless." It is the same Hebrew word used in Ecclesiastes 1:2. Certainly, Abel's life was not meaningless, but it was short, and his name suggests what was to come. Compare Abel's name here and the verse in Ecclesiastes. What connections can you see between the two?

2

SARAH

Her Name Means
"Chieftainness" or "Princess"

HER CHARACTER: Beautiful enough to attract rulers in the ancient world, she could be strong-willed and jealous. Yet Sarah was considered a loyal wife who did what was right and who didn't give in to fear.

KEY SCRIPTURES: Genesis 12:1–20; 16:1–8; 17:1–22; 18:1–15; 21:1–13; Galatians 4:22–31

The name of Abram's wife was Sarai. . . . Now Sarai was barren; she had no children. . . .

God . . . said to Abraham, "As for Sarai your wife, you are no longer to call her Sarai; her name will be Sarah. I will bless her and will surely give you a son by her. I will bless her so that she will be the mother of nations; kings of peoples will come from her."

Abraham fell facedown; he laughed and said to himself, "Will a son be born to a man a hundred years old? Will Sarah bear a child at the age of ninety?" . . .

Then God said, ". . . your wife Sarah will bear you a son, and you will call him Isaac." . . .

Sarah became pregnant and bore a son to Abraham in his old age, at the very time God had promised him. . . .

Sarah said, "God has brought me laughter, and everyone who hears about this will laugh with me." And she added, "Who would have said to Abraham that Sarah would nurse children? Yet I have borne him a son in his old age."

GENESIS 11:29–30; 17:15–17, 19; 21:2, 6–7

Sarah's Life and Times

Names

In Bible times names had a significance they often do not have today. The names the mothers and fathers gave to their children give us a glimpse into their personal experience, sometimes reflecting their emotional responses to a situation. When Sarah was ninety years old, God told her that she and Abraham would finally have the child for whom she had wished for so long. She could hardly believe it! "After I am worn out and my master is old, will I now have this pleasure?" she exclaimed (Genesis 18:12). When her son was born, Sarah named him Isaac, which means "he laughs," and she said, "God has brought me laughter, and everyone who hears about this will laugh with me" (Genesis 21:6).

Perhaps one of the Bible's most poignant scenes is played out when Rachel, in great pain and knowing she was dying, named her son Ben-oni, "son of my trouble." But Jacob, the child's father, loving this little one even in his sorrow, renamed him Benjamin, "son of my right hand" (Genesis 35:16–20). When Hannah's son was born, she named him Samuel, which sounds like the Hebrew for "heard of God," because God had heard her cries for a child. Many of the Old Testament prophets had names that spoke of their mission: Isaiah's name meant "the Lord saves," Obadiah's name meant "servant of the Lord," Nahum's name meant "comfort," and Malachi's name meant "my messenger."

Our Life and Times

Throughout Scripture, God gives to his people names that offer a picture of their significance and worth to him. We are his "treasured possessions" (Exodus 19:5; Malachi 3:17), the "people of his inheritance" (Deuteronomy 4:20), and "sons of the living God" (Hosea 1:10). We are his "friends" (John 15:15). No matter what our given name, God knows it. In love, he calls us to him by our names, and we belong to him (Isaiah 43:1).

Sarah's Legacy in Scripture

Read Genesis 17:15–16; 18:10–15.

1. Both *Sarai* and *Sarah* mean "princess," revealing Sarah's place as a mother of a nation. Do you know the meaning of your name? What significance does its meaning have for you?

2. If you were to ask God to change your name, what would you want your name to be, or mean?

3. Put yourself in Sarah's position. Do you think you might have laughed also? Why or why not?

Read Genesis 21:1–7.

4. God fulfilled his promise to Abraham and Sarah in his time. Describe how you think they felt about God's timing.

5. Have you ever waited for God to fulfill a promise? How did you feel? What did you do?

6. What did Sarah say when she gave birth to Isaac (21:6)? Why do you think she said this?

7. Describe a time in your life when God "brought you laughter."

Read Genesis 16:6; 18:12,15; 21:10.

8. Using these verses, choose five adjectives that describe Sarah. In what ways are you similar to Sarah? In what ways are you unlike her?

9. God used Sarah in spite of her failings, her impatience. How can God use you in spite of your imperfections?

3

HAGAR

Her Name Is Egyptian and
May Mean "Fugitive" or "Immigrant"

HER CHARACTER: A foreigner and slave, she let pride overtake her when she became Abraham's wife. A lonely woman with few resources, she suffered harsh punishment for her mistake. She obeyed God's voice as soon as she heard it and was given a promise that her son would become the father of a great nation.

KEY SCRIPTURES: Genesis 16; 21:8–21; Galatians 4:22–31

After Abram had been living in Canaan ten years, Sarai his wife took her Egyptian maidservant Hagar and gave her to her husband to be his wife. He slept with Hagar, and she conceived. . . .

So Hagar bore Abram a son, and Abram gave the name Ishmael to the son she had borne. . . .

Sarah became pregnant and bore a son to Abraham. . . .

[Isaac] grew and was weaned, and on the day Isaac was weaned Abraham held a great feast. But Sarah saw that the son whom Hagar the Egyptian had borne to Abraham was mocking, and she said to Abraham, "Get rid of that slave woman and her son, for that slave woman's son will never share in the inheritance with my son Isaac." . . .

Abraham took some food and a skin of water and gave them to Hagar. . . .

She went on her way and wandered in the desert. . . .

When the water in the skin was gone, she put the boy under one of the bushes. Then she went off and sat down nearby, about a bowshot away, for she thought, "I cannot watch the boy die." And as she sat there nearby, she began to sob.

God heard the boy crying, and the angel of God called to Hagar from heaven and said to her, "What is the matter, Hagar? Do not be afraid; God has heard the boy crying as he lies there. Lift the boy up and take him by the hand, for I will make him into a great nation."

GENESIS 16:3–4, 15; 21:2, 8–10, 14–18

Hagar's Life and Times

Slavery

Slavery was common practice in ancient Eastern culture, so common that God's laws made provision for its safe and fair practice but not for its destruction. Slaves were obtained in any of a number of ways: captives from war became slaves, particularly virgin women (Numbers 31:7–32); men and women and their children went into slavery to pay debts (Leviticus 25:39); slaves could be purchased (Leviticus 25:44); and sometimes slavery was even voluntary, as when a male slave who could have gone free remained in servitude to stay with a wife he loved (Exodus 21:2–6).

Hagar, an Egyptian, probably became a slave to Abraham and Sarah when they left Egypt (Genesis 12:20). Leaving her homeland behind, she made herself useful and proved herself trustworthy, thereby becoming Sarah's maidservant, a position of some importance in the household.

Sarah must have had some confidence and perhaps even affection for Hagar to want her to be the surrogate mother of her son. Such practices were common in that day. Infertile women urged their husbands to sleep with their maidservants to gain a child and heir for the family. Female slaves were often made the concubines or wives of the master or one of his sons. Their children became the property and sometimes the heirs of their masters. As female slaves, they had no choice in the matter. They had no rights and no one to defend them.

Our Life and Times

Many women today are in a position similar to Hagar's. They may not be actual slaves, but they are in positions of weakness, with no one to defend them. No one except God. The same God who defended Hagar and heard the cries of her son in the desert hears the cries of helpless women and their children today. When we are at our weakest, God is at his best, ready to step in and say to us as he said to Hagar, "Do not be afraid" (Genesis 21:17).

Hagar's Legacy in Scripture

Read Genesis 16:1–12.

1. Sarah's proposition (16:2) was a customary one of that day. Hagar had little say, but she must have had some reaction to the proposition. What do you think Hagar's reaction might have been?

2. What reaction do you have when you find yourself in a situation over which you have no control? How can God help you when you are in such a position?

3. Why do you think the pregnant Hagar began to despise Sarah (16:4)?

4. The area to which Hagar ran away was probably barren and sparsely populated (16:7). Describe how desperate she must have felt to run away from a difficult but safe situation to the "desert."

5. Have you ever been that desperate? What were the circumstances?

6. God's words to Hagar here are words of assurance but also of prophecy. Her descendants would be "too numerous to count" (16:10), but the son through whom those descendants would come would "be a wild donkey of a man" (16:12). What picture of Ishmael does that put into your mind? What kind of a man do you think he was?

7. Do you have family members who, like Ishmael, "live in hostility" (16:12)? How do you respond to them? What can you do to improve your relationship with them?

Read Genesis 21:8–21.

8. Even though Hagar and Ishmael were outcasts and alone, God lovingly cared for them. Describe how you think Hagar felt when she laid Ishmael down and went away because she "could not watch the boy die." How did God meet her needs?

9. In what ways has God met your needs when you were despairing and alone?

10. Are you in a desperate situation right now? Read Genesis 21:19 again. Might there be a "well" to which you can go for sustenance, if only you could see it? Ask God to open your eyes to the way out of your situation just as he opened Hagar's eyes and aided her in her desperation.

4

LOT'S WIFE

HER CHARACTER: She was a prosperous woman who may have been more attached to the good life than was good for her. Though there is no indication she participated in the sin of Sodom, her story implies that she had learned to tolerate it and that her heart had become divided as a result.

KEY SCRIPTURES: Genesis 18:16–19:29; Luke 17:28–33

With the coming of dawn, the angels urged Lot, saying, "Hurry! Take your wife and your two daughters who are here, or you will be swept away when the city is punished."

When he hesitated, the men grasped his hand and the hands of his wife and of his two daughters and led them safely out of the city, for the LORD was merciful to them. As soon as they had brought them out, one of them said, "Flee for your lives! Don't look back, and don't stop anywhere in the plain! Flee to the mountains or you will be swept away!" . . .

By the time Lot reached Zoar, the sun had risen over the land. Then the LORD rained down burning sulfur on Sodom and Gomorrah—from the LORD out of the heavens. Thus he overthrew those cities and the entire plain, including all those living in the cities—and also the vegetation in the land. But Lot's wife looked back, and she became a pillar of salt.

GENESIS 19:15–17, 23–26

Lot's Wife's Life and Times

S a l t

Lot's wife is remembered less for who she was—wife, mother, daughter, sister—than for what she became—a pillar of salt. Just one irresistible but forbidden glance back at what was happening behind her, and she turned into salt. Salt! One of the world's most common, and most used, chemicals.

Palestine, in fact, possessed rich salt depositories, which accounted for such place names as the Salt Sea (also known as the Dead Sea), the Valley of Salt, and the City of Salt. The Romans probably looked on Israel as a worthy conquest simply because of the salt available there.

The Hebrews used salt to season food: "Is tasteless food eaten without salt?" (Job 6:6). Hebrew women rubbed their newborn babies with salt or washed them in it: "On the day you were born your cord was not cut, nor were you washed with water to make you clean, nor were you rubbed with salt" (Ezekiel 16:4). Salt was a required supplement to any Old Testament grain sacrifice: "Season all your grain offerings with salt" (Leviticus 2:13).

Our Life and Times

The word *salt* is used only six times in the entire New Testament, all of them symbolic. Jesus said to remember that as a believer we are the salt of the earth (Matthew 5:13; Mark 9:50; Luke 14:34). Our attitudes and actions can cleanse and season and purify our surroundings. When we respond graciously to someone who is ungracious, we season our world with salt. When we treat an irritable child with kindness, we season our homes with salt. When we comfort the hurt, console the lonely, encourage the discouraged, or calm the unsettled, we season our world with salt. As followers of Christ, we're saltshakers (we hope full ones!), busy sprinkling our world with the salt that flavors life.

Lot's Wife's Legacy in Scripture

Read Genesis 19:1–8.

1. Lot invited these men to stay in his home without even consulting his wife. What sort of home do you think Lot's wife must have made for him and his children?

2. How do you respond when someone you live with invites a guest over unexpectedly? Are you gracious? Frazzled? Antagonized?

3. What do you think of Lot's suggestion that he give his daughters to the raiders rather than his guests (19:8)? What reaction do you think Lot's wife might have had?

4. Why would Lot offer such a thing? Keep in mind that, according to ancient culture, in opening his house to these guests Lot guaranteed not only their comfort but their safety.

5. Do you think the time you are living in is more or less degenerate than the times recorded here? Why?

Read Genesis 19:15–17, 26.

6. Why do you think Lot hesitated? What might he have been thinking?

7. When have you hesitated to do something you knew God wanted you to do? Why did you hesitate? What happened?

8. Even though warned not to do so, Lot's wife couldn't resist looking back. Why do you think she turned? Was she sad? Scared? Curious?

9. In Lot's wife, we can see ourselves looking back, regretting decisions made, mourning lost opportunities, yearning for ended relationships. Because we're looking behind us, we can't see what is before us. We may not turn into a pillar of salt, but we'll end up stuck in one place. Do you spend a lot of time looking back? How can you leave the past behind, enjoy the present, and plan for the future?

5

REBEKAH

Her Name Probably Means
"Loop" or "Tie"

HER CHARACTER: Hard-working and generous, her faith was so great that she left her home forever to marry a man she had never seen or met. Yet she played favorites with her sons and failed to trust God fully for the promise he had made.

KEY SCRIPTURES: Genesis 24; 25:19–34; 26:1–28

꙼

"When I [Abraham's servant] came to the spring today, I said, 'O LORD, God of my master Abraham, if you will, please grant success to the journey on which I have come. See, I am standing beside this spring; if a maiden comes out to draw water and I say to her, "Please let me drink a little water from your jar," and if she says to me, "Drink, and I'll draw water for your camels too," let her be the one the LORD has chosen for my master's son [Isaac].'

"Before I finished praying in my heart, Rebekah came out, with her jar on her shoulder. She went down to the spring and drew water, and I said to her, 'Please give me a drink.'

"She quickly lowered her jar from her shoulder and said, 'Drink, and I'll water your camels too.' So I drank, and she watered the camels also."

. . . Then the servant told Isaac all he had done. Isaac brought [Rebekah] into the tent of his mother Sarah, and he married Rebekah. So she became his wife, and he loved her; and Isaac was comforted after his mother's death.

GENESIS 24:42–46; 66–67

Rebekah's Life and Times

Jewelry

> "Then I put the ring in her nose and the bracelets on her arms."...Then the servant brought out gold and silver jewelry and articles of clothing and gave them to Rebekah.
>
> GENESIS 24:47, 53

A nose ring! Often taken as a sign of rebellious youth today, a nose ring was an acceptable form of adornment in ancient times. When Abraham's servant realized Rebekah was the woman Isaac was to marry, he immediately got out the jewels he had brought along for the occasion. He gave her two gold bracelets and a gold nose ring. Rebekah quickly slipped the jewelry on and ran home with shining eyes to tell her family what had occurred.

A nose ring is mentioned only two other times in Scripture—in Proverbs 11 and Ezekiel 16. In Ezekiel 16, God is describing in allegorical terms how much he loves the city of Jerusalem. He lovingly bathes her, then dresses her in wonderfully rich clothing and soft leather sandals. He then tenderly adorns her with jewelry. "I put bracelets on your arms and a necklace around your neck, and I put a ring on your nose, earrings on your ears and a beautiful crown on your head. So you were adorned with gold and silver" (Ezekiel 16:11–13).

The Old Testament mentions jewels and jewelry numerous times. Women and men both wore earrings (Exodus 32:2). They also commonly wore "armlets, bracelets, signet rings, earrings and necklaces" (Numbers 31:50). The Israelites took most of their jewelry from others while at war; gold and silver and gemstones are often listed among the booty taken during a raid. Second Samuel 8:11 records the fact that David gained enormous amounts of gold and silver and bronze when he conquered the nations surrounding Israel. He dedicated all of it to the Lord, and his son Solomon used it to build the fabulous temple in Jerusalem. Believe it or not, Solomon had so much gold in his kingdom that he "made silver and gold as common in Jerusalem as stones" (2 Chronicles 1:15).

The New Testament mentions jewelry specifically only once. Peter urges women to pay more attention to their inner beauty than their outward beauty (1 Peter 3:3–4). He wants them—and us—to remember that outer beauty fades away, but inner beauty grows more attractive with each year.

Our Life and Times

Tomorrow morning, when you put your rings on your fingers, also put on a spirit of peace. When you put your earrings on your ears, put them on with a cheerful attitude. When you clasp your necklace around your neck, clasp a sweet spirit to your heart also. The jewelry you wear won't make much difference in your day. But the spirit you wear will.

Rebekah's Legacy in Scripture

Read Genesis 24:12–27.

1. What does this first information about young Rebekah tell you about her looks and her character?

2. How are you like Rebekah? How are you different from her?

Read Genesis 24:28–58.

3. In these verses Abraham's servant tells Rebekah's family how he met her, emphasizing the Lord's blessing and involvement throughout. How does Rebekah's family respond?

4. Three simple words (24:58) changed Rebekah's life forever. Who was she like in her willingness to go where she had never been before?

5. How would you react if God called you away from home and family? What would have to happen to make you obey?

Read Genesis 24:67; 25:28.

6. These are some of the sweetest words about marriage found in the Bible. In your own words, describe what you think Isaac and Rebekah's marriage was like in these early days.

7. Verse 28 expresses one of the saddest thoughts about parenting found in the Bible. Describe how you think their parents' favoritism affected Jacob and Esau and their relationship.

8. Many children grow up thinking their parents favored one sibling or another. If you have children, how can you avoid such thinking in them?

Read Genesis 27:1–28:9.

9. Why do you think Rebekah resorted to trickery to gain the promise given to her when she was pregnant?

10. Describe how you think Rebekah might have felt ten years later. Do you think she regretted her actions?

11. How are Rebekah's actions like those of her mother-in-law, Sarah?

12. The story of Rebekah is rich and colorful. In one sentence summarize what you would like to learn from her life.

6

RACHEL

Her Name Means "Ewe"

HER CHARACTER: Manipulated by her father, she had little say over her own life circumstances and relationships. But rather than dealing creatively with a difficult situation, she behaved like a perpetual victim, responding to sin with yet more sin, making things worse by competing with her sister and deceiving her father in return.

KEY SCRIPTURES: Genesis 29–35; Jeremiah 31:15; Matthew 2:18

Now Laban had two daughters; the name of the older was Leah, and the name of the younger was Rachel. . . . Rachel was lovely in form, and beautiful. Jacob was in love with Rachel and said, "I'll work for you seven years in return for your younger daughter Rachel."

. . . So Jacob served seven years to get Rachel, but they seemed like only a few days to him because of his love for her.

. . . So Laban brought together all the people of the place and gave a feast. But when evening came, he took his daughter Leah and gave her to Jacob, and Jacob lay with her. . . .

When morning came, there was Leah! So Jacob said to Laban, "What is this you have done to me? I served you for Rachel, didn't I? Why have you deceived me?"

Laban replied, "It is not our custom here to give the younger daughter in marriage before the older one. Finish this daughter's bridal week; then we will give you the younger one also, in return for another seven years of work."

And Jacob did so. He finished the week with Leah, and then Laban gave him his daughter Rachel to be his wife. . . . Jacob lay with Rachel also, and he loved Rachel more than Leah. And he worked for Laban another seven years.

When the LORD saw that Leah was not loved, he opened her womb, but Rachel was barren. . . .

When Rachel saw that she was not bearing Jacob any children . . . she said to Jacob, "Give me children, or I'll die!" . . .

Then God remembered Rachel; he listened to her and opened her womb. She became pregnant and gave birth to a son and . . . named him Joseph. . . .

Rachel began to give birth [to another child] and had great difficulty. . . . As she breathed her last—for she was dying—she named her son Ben-Oni. But his father named him Benjamin.

GENESIS 29:16–18, 20, 22–23, 25–28, 30–31; 30:1, 22–24; 35:16, 18

Rachel's Life and Times

Menstrual Cycles

Rachel said to her father, 'Don't be angry, my lord, that I cannot stand up in your presence; I'm having my period.' So [Laban] searched, but could not find the household gods" (Genesis 31:35). Rachel's words here are the only mention in Scripture of a typical monthly menstrual cycle, other than the ceremonial laws covering menstruation found in Leviticus and referred to again in Ezekiel.

Rachel knew without a doubt that her ploy would successfully deter her father. By claiming to have her period, she not only kept the false gods she had stolen, she kept her very life, since Jacob had promised to kill whoever had stolen the idols from Laban.

During the time a Hebrew woman had her period, she was considered "unclean." This is not surprising considering the untidy nature of a monthly flow, especially in these days, long before the invention of feminine sanitary products. But the laws covered more than the monthly period itself. Those who touched a woman at this time, even by chance, became unclean until evening. Wherever the woman slept or sat also became unclean. Anyone who touched her bedding or her seat was considered unclean until they washed their clothes, bathed, and waited until evening.

A woman was considered unclean for seven days, the normal length of a woman's period. She then customarily bathed to cleanse herself. This is probably the bath that Bathsheba was taking when spotted by King David (2 Samuel 11:2–4). Since she had just had her period, David could be sure Bathsheba's child was his when she told him she was pregnant.

The natural flow of a woman's period didn't require sacrifices for her to be cleansed; merely bathing and waiting for a prescribed time was enough. A longer, less natural flow, usually caused by some infection or disease, required a sacrifice in order for the woman to be clean. Neither implied any moral failing on the part of the woman, but since blood was seen as a source of life, anything surrounding it became an important part of ceremonial law.

Our Life and Times

Many women consider their period, and the discomfort and irritability that often come along with it, a monthly trial—something women must bear, and men, lucky creatures, are spared. However, it is only through this particular function of her body that a woman can reproduce and carry a child. Although at times messy, at times a nuisance, at times downright painful, only through this process does a woman have the opportunity afforded to no man—the opportunity to bear new life. And in so doing, to be uniquely linked to the Creator of all life.

Rachel's Legacy in Scripture

Read Genesis 29:30; 30:1.

1. How do you think most women would respond to the situation in which Rachel found herself (29:30)? With love and concern for her unloved sister? Or with a spirit of superiority and pride?

2. The agony expressed by Rachel's words in Genesis 30:1 has been experienced by many women over the centuries. How did Rachel's close relationship with Leah increase her pain? Is there any way their relationship could have eased her pain instead?

Compare Genesis 29:30–31 and 30:1.

3. These two sisters each had something the other wanted. What did Rachel have that Leah wanted? What did Leah have that Rachel wanted?

4. Discontentment is an insidious thing, trapping us into thinking that which was enough is no longer enough, and that which was satisfying is no longer satisfying. Do you ever feel discontent because you don't "have it all"? What can you do to resist such sentiments?

Read Genesis 31:19, 30–34.

5. Why would Rachel even have such idols? Why do you think she hid them from her father?

6. When have you been in a situation that caused you to lie or cheat to protect yourself or someone else? Describe it. What could/should you have done differently?

Read Genesis 35:16–20.

7. Given the fact that they were on a journey, describe in your own words the situation under which Rachel likely gave birth.

8. It's one of the paradoxes of life, revealed here in this tragic story of Rachel's death, that what we most want from life we often can only gain by giving up something else that's equally important to us. Can you think of an instance in your own life in which gaining something you wanted required giving up something else?

9. Jacob renamed his new son Benjamin, which means "son of my right hand." What does this new name reveal about Jacob's hope for the future?

7

LEAH

Her Name May Mean
"Impatient" or "Wild Cow"

HER CHARACTER: Capable of both strong and enduring love, she was a faithful mother and wife. Manipulated by her father, she became jealous of her sister, with whom, it seems, she never reconciled.

KEY SCRIPTURES: Genesis 29–35; Ruth 4:11

Notes

Now Laban had two daughters; the name of the older was Leah, and the name of the younger was Rachel. Leah had weak eyes, but Rachel was lovely in form, and beautiful. Jacob was in love with Rachel. . . .

When evening came, [Laban] took his daughter Leah and gave her to Jacob, and Jacob lay with her. . . .

When morning came, there was Leah! So Jacob said to Laban, "What is this you have done to me? I served you for Rachel, didn't I? Why have you deceived me?" . . .

When the LORD saw that Leah was not loved, he opened her womb, but Rachel was barren.

——— GENESIS 29:16–18, 23, 25, 31 ———

Leah's Life and Times

Marriage Customs

The customs of marriage in ancient biblical times were far different from our own modern customs. Seldom did a man or woman marry for love. Jacob is a notable exception when he expresses his love for Rachel and his desire to marry her.

Usually the bride and groom were very young when they married. The bride was often only around twelve and the groom around thirteen. Their marriage was arranged by parents, and their consent was neither requested nor required. Even so, such marriages could prove to be love matches, like that between Isaac and Rebekah.

The marriage ceremony itself was usually very short, but the festivities connected with it could go on for many days. The groom dressed in colorful clothing and set out just before sunset, with his friends and attendants and musicians, for the home of the bride's parents. There the bride would be waiting, washed and perfumed and bedecked in an elaborate dress and jewels. The bride and groom then led the marriage procession through the village streets, accompanied by music and torchbearers, to the groom's parents' home. The feasting and celebration began that night and often continued for seven days.

God's design for marriage to be between one husband and one wife often was not practiced in early biblical times. Jacob married both Rachel and her sister, Leah, a practice that was later forbidden by law (Leviticus 18:18). Leah shared her husband Jacob with not only her sister, Rachel, but also with their maids, Zilpah and Bilhah. (For more on Jacob and his wives and children, see the chart on page 232.) Although polygamy was less common after the Exodus from Egypt, Gideon had a number of wives (Judges 8:30), and, of course, Solomon had many (1 Kings 11:3). But, as the New Testament indicates, a union between one husband and one wife continues to be God's design and desire (1 Timothy 3:2, 12; Titus 1:6).

Our Life and Times

Marriage customs today may differ in many ways from those of Bible times. Few marriages are arranged by parents. Instead, the couples themselves make the decision to marry. Most marriages still involve a procession; however, it's most often down a church aisle rather than from the groom's home to the bride's. No matter how much is different, however, one thing remains the same. The start of married life is still a season of celebration and rejoicing.

Leah's Legacy in Scripture

Read Genesis 29:30–34.

1. Pick one word you think best describes how Leah felt about this marriage to Jacob.

2. Many women today have husbands who love something more than their wives: job, position, money, sports. Many things other than another woman can put a wife in Leah's position. If you know someone who is a "Leah," pray daily for her and be an encouragement to her when given the opportunity.

3. Leah is an unparalleled example of God's willingness to give "beauty" for "ashes" (see Isaiah 61:1–3). How has God worked this way in your life? How has he worked this way in the lives of your friends or relatives?

4. In Genesis 29:32–34, Leah expresses her desire for Jacob's affection, an affection she knew she didn't have. In your own words, describe how Leah probably felt and acted toward Jacob. What do you think Jacob's reaction was?

5. Have you ever felt unloved by your husband, your parents, or someone else? How did you feel and act? What is your only possible source of comfort when you desperately want a love you don't have?

Read Genesis 49:29–31.

6. Jacob was buried next to the wife he loved less rather than next to the wife he loved more. What does this say not only about Leah's position as a wife, but also as a mother of the Israelites?

7. Although Leah was, of course, unaware of the position she was awarded in death, what do these verses continue to reveal about God's involvement in her life?

8. Leah had a full life with many sons and wealth. However, she is best known for what she didn't have: the love of her husband. God noticed what she did have but also what she lacked. What one thing do you want to learn from Leah and from her God?

8

TAMAR, DAUGHTER-IN-LAW OF JUDAH

Her Name Means "Date Tree" or "Palm Tree"

HER CHARACTER: Driven by one overwhelming need, she sacrificed her reputation and nearly her life to achieve her goals.

KEY SCRIPTURES: Genesis 38; Matthew 1:3

Notes

Judah got a wife for Er ... and her name was Tamar. But Er ... was wicked in the LORD's sight; so the LORD put him to death.

Then Judah said to Onan, "Lie with your brother's wife and ... produce offspring for your brother." But Onan knew that the offspring would not be his; so whenever he lay with his brother's wife, he spilled his semen on the ground to keep from producing offspring for his brother. What he did was wicked in the LORD's sight; so he put him to death also.

Judah then said to his daughter-in-law Tamar, "Live as a widow in your father's house until my son Shelah grows up." For he thought, "He may die too, just like his brothers." So Tamar went to live in her father's house.

... When Tamar was told, "Your father-in-law is on his way to Timnah to shear his sheep," she took off her widow's clothes, covered herself with a veil to disguise herself. ... For she saw that, though Shelah had now grown up, she had not been given to him as his wife.

When Judah saw her, he thought she was a prostitute. ... Not realizing that she was his daughter-in-law, he went over to her by the roadside and said, "Come now, let me sleep with you." ...

So he ... slept with her, and she became pregnant by him. ...

... When the time came for [Tamar] to give birth, there were twin boys in her womb.

——— GENESIS 38:6–11, 13–16, 18, 27 ———

Tamar's Life and Times

Prostitution

As abhorrent as it seems to us, prostitution was actually an expression of worship in the ancient Near East. Pagan peoples often believed that fertility gods granted blessings to those who practiced cultic prostitution. The sacrifices and the payments for the use of a cult prostitute brought huge amounts of money into the coffers of the god or goddess being worshiped. The sexual intercourse itself symbolized the hoped-for fertility and abundance of the harvest.

Judah, a widower who had only recently "recovered from his grief" (Genesis 38:12), traveled to Timnah during sheep-shearing time to watch his own sheep being sheared. It may be that when he saw Tamar he took her for a shrine prostitute and had intercourse with her to ensure a good crop of wool. This, of course, in no way justifies Judah's act, but it does shed some light on his possible motives.

Shrine prostitutes usually kept themselves heavily veiled before and during the act of intercourse, an attempt to create the illusion that the participant was actually engaging in the sexual act with the goddess herself. This practice worked in Tamar's favor, giving her the perfect disguise so that her father-in-law would never recognize her.

Prostitution was the imagery used often by the biblical prophets to describe Israel's waywardness, their proneness to follow false gods. They saw God as the husband of Israel, her keeper and her true love. Whenever the Israelites turned from the true God to false gods, they "prostituted" themselves. It is a strong picture, but an accurate one of turning away from the God who truly loved them and was willing to care for them and watch over them, if only they would remain true to him.

Our Life and Times

Tamar's story takes us by surprise, repulses us. We recoil from the sordid details of prostitution and find little to inspire us. Yet stories like Tamar's are what make the Bible so believable. Who would ever invent such a thing, then record it not only in the historical narrative but also in the lineage of the Messiah? Only the God of eternal surprises—the God who takes the unfit, the desperate, and the profane, and uses them to his eternal and holy purposes.

Tamar's Legacy in Scripture

Read Genesis 38.

1. Onan was supposed to father children through Tamar for his brother, Er. This is the same act as that of the "kinsman-redeemer" found in the book of Ruth. The closest of kin was to father a child to carry on the line of the deceased husband. Although the act may seem offensive to us today, what do you think God's purpose was in decreeing such a plan?

2. None of the men in Tamar's life fulfilled their responsibilities to her, including her father-in-law, Judah (38:11). Describe how you think Tamar must have been feeling throughout the course of these events. Angry? Ignored? Dishonored? Belittled? Ashamed?

3. Why was Tamar so desperate to have a child?

4. Are you, or is someone you know, desperate to have children? How do the ordeals of infertility today compare to what Tamar was willing to endure in ancient times?

5. What do you think of Judah's response to the news that Tamar was pregnant (38:24)? Was it a double standard for him to condemn her actions but not his own?

6. Do such double standards still exist today? How? Are they as common as they were, say, ten or twenty years ago?

7. When you consider what Tamar did in offering herself disguised as a prostitute to her father-in-law, do his words in verse 26 surprise you? Why? Explain what Judah meant by these words.

8. The story of Tamar is a difficult one to digest. There is simply no way to assimilate what she did with our current way of thinking. Why would such a story ever be included in the inspired Scriptures?

Read Matthew 1:3.

9. What does Tamar's inclusion in the lineage of Christ tell you about God's power to bring good out of tragic events?

10. How has God worked good out of the bad things that have happened to you or to someone you know?

POTIPHAR'S
WIFE

HER CHARACTER: The wife of a prosperous and influential Egyptian, she was unfaithful and vindictive, ready to lie in order to protect herself and ruin an innocent man.

KEY SCRIPTURE: Genesis 39

ン

[Joseph] lived in the house of his Egyptian master. . . . Potiphar put him in charge of his household. . . .

Now Joseph was well-built and handsome, and after a while his master's wife took notice of Joseph and said, "Come to bed with me!"

But he refused. . . .

One day he went into the house to attend to his duties, and none of the household servants was inside. [Potiphar's wife] caught him by his cloak and said, "Come to bed with me!" But he left his cloak in her hand and ran out of the house. . . .

She kept his cloak beside her until his master came home. Then she told him this story: "That Hebrew slave you brought us came to me to make sport of me. But as soon as I screamed for help, he left his cloak beside me and ran out of the house."

When his master heard the story his wife told him . . . [he] took [Joseph] and put him in prison.

GENESIS 39:2, 4, 6–8, 11–12, 16–20

Potiphar's Wife's Life and Times

Egyptian Life

In the ancient world, Egypt was considered the world's breadbasket. The Nile River regularly overflowed its banks, depositing rich soil and moisture along the river valley—a perfect place for abundant crops to grow. But fertile ground in Egypt could be found only as far as the Nile reached, a division so pronounced one could literally stand with one foot on rich soil and the other in sand.

Whenever famine struck other parts of the Middle East, the starving inhabitants would hurry to Egypt for food: "Now there was a famine in the land, and Abram went down to Egypt to live there for a while because the famine was severe" (Genesis 12:10). "When Jacob learned that there was grain in Egypt, he said to his sons, 'Why do you just keep looking at each other?' He continued, 'I have heard that there is grain in Egypt. Go down there and buy some for us, so that we may live and not die'" (Genesis 42:1–2).

In addition to serving as the world's breadbasket, Egypt was the site of many impressive building projects. Some of the pharaohs constructed enormous tombs in which they and their families were to be ushered into the afterlife. Egyptians believed that their bodies were the eternal houses for their souls; therefore they became adept at mummification, preserving the bodies of the dead so thoroughly that some have survived until today.

Egypt's building projects were completed at tremendous human cost. Egyptian pharaohs forced the Hebrews into slavery, using them to complete their temples and tombs. Most likely the Hebrew oppression took place during the Nineteenth Dynasty of Egypt under the Pharaoh Ramses. Officials during that time have left behind their notations of the numbers of bricks made each day as well as their complaints at the scarcity of straw for the bricks.

Temples and tombs were filled with furniture of ebony and ivory, elegant vases, and copper tools, as well as gold jewelry and ornaments. Artisans etched beautifully drawn scenes of daily life on the walls of tombs to provide comfort for the one buried there.

As the wife of a high-ranking Egyptian official, Potiphar's wife likely led a life of relative ease and prosperity. According to the story in Genesis 39, Potiphar's household and business matters prospered because of Joseph's influence, and "the blessing of the Lord was on everything Potiphar had, both in the house and in the field" (Genesis 39:5).

Our Life and Times

Notes

The story of seduction and desire is as old as history. Scripture doesn't record if Joseph found Potiphar's wife attractive and desirable. That detail could be considered superfluous since he rejected her because he "could not do such a wicked thing and sin against God." The jaded, older Egyptian woman and her desires provide a stunning backdrop for Joseph's purity, making Joseph and his choice to walk in a righteous manner all the more clear and attractive.

Potiphar's Wife's Legacy in Scripture

Read Genesis 39:2–20.

1. What character trait was Potiphar's wife lacking? Why do you think she was attracted to Joseph, beyond the fact that he was "well-built and handsome"?

2. Like Potiphar's wife, what do you wish you had that you don't have? Is it something you shouldn't have? If it is, ask God to help you root it out of your spirit.

3. Where do you suppose Joseph got his knowledge of right and wrong and his ability to reject sin (39:9)? What do you think Joseph's life might have been like if he had given in to Potiphar's wife?

4. What legacy has sin or a rejection of sin left in your life?

5. Why do you think Joseph avoided contact with Potiphar's wife (39:10)? Contrast how these two characters responded to temptation.

6. If temptation of a certain kind keeps coming into your life, how do you respond?

7. The story Potiphar's wife told her husband (39:17–18) was just that, a story, a piece of fiction. Describe what you think Joseph's feelings might have been when he heard the "story."

8. Like Potiphar's wife, have you ever accused someone unjustly? What were the circumstances? How did you deal with the sin involved and correct the wrong?

10

THE MOTHERS OF MOSES

JOCHEBED

Her Name Means "The Lord Is Glory"

HER CHARACTER: Her fierce love for her son, coupled with her faith, enabled her to act heroically in the midst of great oppression.

KEY SCRIPTURES: Exodus 2:1–10; Hebrews 11:23

PHARAOH'S DAUGHTER

HER CHARACTER: The Jewish people honor men and women whom they designate as "righteous Gentiles." These are people who, though nonbelievers, have assisted God's people in some significant way. Surely, Pharaoh's daughter should top the list of righteous Gentiles, courageously and compassionately delivering a child from death, a child who would one day act as Israel's great deliverer.

KEY SCRIPTURE: Exodus 2:1–10

❧

Pharaoh gave this order to all his people: "Every [Hebrew] boy that is born you must throw into the Nile. . . ."

Now a man of the house of Levi married a Levite woman, and she became pregnant and gave birth to a son. When she saw that he was a fine child, she hid him for three months. But when she could hide him no longer, she . . .

placed the child in [a basket] and put it among the reeds along the bank of the Nile. His sister stood at a distance to see what would happen to him.

Then Pharaoh's daughter went down to the Nile to bathe. . . . She saw the basket among the reeds . . . and saw the baby. He was crying, and she felt sorry for him. "This is one of the Hebrew babies," she said.

Then [the baby's] sister asked Pharaoh's daughter, "Shall I go and get one of the Hebrew women to nurse the baby for you?"

"Yes, go," she answered. And the girl went and got the baby's mother. . . . So the woman took the baby and nursed him.

——————   EXODUS 1:22; 2:1–9   ——————

Notes

Moses' Mothers' Life and Times

Baskets

Such an ordinary object, used to such extraordinary purpose. Imagine with what love and care Jochebed coated the papyrus basket with tar and pitch before placing her precious son within it. Few baskets throughout the centuries likely received as loving and careful a touch.

Baskets were just one of the many types of vessels used to store and carry various items in the ancient world. In the home, women used baskets to store household items as well as fruit and bread. Brick makers carried their clay in baskets. Travelers used them to carry the supplies they needed for their journey. Priests used baskets to store the bread and wafers that were a part of worship in the tabernacle (Exodus 29:3, 23, 32).

Typically made from plant material—leaves, twigs, or stalks—baskets came in a variety of shapes and sizes. The smallest could be carried in one hand. Baskets just a bit larger were carried on the back or on the head and were often used to hold provisions on a trip. The disciples used twelve of these large baskets to gather up the leftovers at the feeding of the five thousand (Matthew 14:20). An even larger basket was used to let Paul escape out of a window in the wall at Damascus (Acts 9:25).

Our Life and Times

God's use of the ordinary to bring about the extraordinary is as much in evidence here in the early events of Exodus as anywhere in Scripture. His tendency to bring about his will through ordinary items, ordinary people, and ordinary events is no less at work today than it was in Jochebed's. If we look for the signs of his presence, we are sure to discover them.

Moses' Mothers' Legacy in Scripture

Read Exodus 2:1–10.

1. In your own words describe the events of verses 1 and 2. Look behind the scenes. How do you think the family kept the baby quiet? If a close neighbor heard the newborn's cries, what do you think he or she would have done? What if that neighbor had herself just lost a newborn to Pharaoh's decrees? Why at three months could Jochebed "hide him no longer"?

2. How do you think you would have reacted in these circumstances? Like Jochebed? Like the other mothers?

3. The events in verses 3 and 4 go straight to a mother's heart. How do you think Jochebed felt as she walked away from the river?

4. What is most obvious about Pharaoh's daughter from verses 5 and 6?

5. Why do you suppose she was allowed to disobey her father's harsh edict?

6. Compare Exodus 2:9 and 10. What conflicting emotions do you think Jochebed must have felt?

Reread Exodus 2:10.

7. What is the significance of the words "he [Moses] became her son"?

8. What purpose of God was at work here?

Read Hebrews 11:23.

9. This verse says that Moses' mother and father acted "by faith." Their one goal was to protect and save their child. Fear for our children's safety—for their spiritual and physical lives—seems to be an inescapable part of parenting. What part does faith play in child rearing? What is your greatest fear for your child? How can you "by faith" respond to your fears?

11

MIRIAM

Her Name May Mean "Bitterness"

HER CHARACTER: Even as a young girl, she showed fortitude and wisdom. A leader of God's people at a crucial moment in history, she led the celebration after crossing the Red Sea and spoke God's word to his people, sharing their forty-year journey through the wilderness.

KEY SCRIPTURES: Exodus 2:1–10; 15:20–21; Numbers 12:1–15

When Pharaoh's horses, chariots and horsemen went into the sea, the LORD brought the waters of the sea back over them, but the Israelites walked through the sea on dry ground. Then Miriam the prophetess, Aaron's sister, took a tambourine in her hand, and all the women followed her, with tambourines and dancing. . . .

Miriam and Aaron began to talk against Moses because of his Cushite wife, for he had married a Cushite. "Has the LORD spoken only through Moses?" they asked. "Hasn't he also spoken through us?" And the LORD heard this.

(Now Moses was a very humble man, more humble than anyone else on the face of the earth.)

At once the LORD said to Moses, Aaron and Miriam, "Come out to the Tent of Meeting, all three of you." So the three of them came out. Then the LORD came down in a pillar of cloud; he . . . summoned Aaron and Miriam [and] said . . . "Why then were you not afraid to speak against my servant Moses?"

The anger of the LORD burned against them, and he left them.

When the cloud lifted from above the Tent, there stood Miriam—leprous, like snow. . . .

So Miriam was confined outside the camp for seven days, and the people did not move on till she was brought back.

EXODUS 15:19–20; NUMBERS 12:1–5, 8–10, 15

Miriam's Life and Times

Dancing

In biblical times, people danced to celebrate happy events and to praise God. Dancing in Scripture is always linked to joy and happiness. The presence of mourning means the absence of dancing (Lamentations 5:15), and there is a time for both (Ecclesiastes 3:4).

The very first mention of dancing in Scripture is when Miriam led the Israelite women in a dance that celebrated God's miraculous defeat of the Egyptians at the Red Sea. Imagine, if you can, the emotions of these women as they ran between the walls of water of the Red Sea, Egyptian chariots right behind them. Fearful for their lives, they breathlessly reached the eastern shore, turning around to see the waters come crashing in to drown the Egyptians and their horses—a narrow, frightening escape.

Then, quickly, fear gave way to a thrill of excitement. They were free! When Miriam went by with a tambourine, singing a song of praise to God, the women's feet moved to her rhythm, their voices joined her song, and they danced!

The Hebrews danced in worship, often in praise of God for his deliverance from enemies (1 Samuel 18:6; Psalm 149:3). They danced to celebrate happy events, like weddings and the return of loved ones (Luke 15:25). Hebrew men and women didn't dance together. The men usually danced alone, as David did before the ark (2 Samuel 6:14), while the women danced together.

There is some evidence that dancing was a part of the worship of the early Christian church. But according to several early Christian writers, it soon degenerated and no longer expressed a pure praise of the Lord. Before long it was banned.

Our Life and Times

Just as Miriam and the women couldn't help but dance with joy, so when God does a wonderful work in our lives we sometimes respond in much the same manner: our faces break into smiles, our hands are lifted up, and our feet can't remain still! Certainly the God who created the human body delights in the pure use of that beautiful instrument to offer praise to him.

Miriam's Legacy in Scripture

Read Exodus 15:19–21.

1. Describe what you think Miriam and the other women of Israel were thinking and feeling as they walked through the Red Sea. After they made it safely through, why do you think they chose to dance to express their praise?

2. How do you think you would have felt in that situation? Would you have danced? Or would you have used some other form of praise to God? If so, what?

Read Numbers 12:1–15.

3. What do you think Aaron and Miriam had against Moses' "Cushite" wife? Do you think his wife was the real problem? What was the real problem, the real reason for their attack?

4. Contrast what verses 1–2 reveal about Miriam and Aaron with what verse 3 reveals about Moses. In what ways are you like Miriam and Aaron? How are you like Moses?

5. In verses 4–9 the Lord appears in the pillar of cloud to Moses, Aaron, and Miriam. He then singles out Aaron and Miriam and speaks to them. Why is he so angry with them?

6. Why do you think Miriam was singled out for the punishment of leprosy and not Aaron?

7. How do you think Miriam's punishment affected Aaron?

8. Have you ever been in a situation where one person was punished for the wrongdoing of several? How did that make you feel?

9. What do you think Miriam was feeling and thinking when she was outside the camp for those seven days (12:14–15)? What would go through your mind if you were in Miriam's position?

10. Even when we are forgiven, we sometimes still have to pay the price for our sins. What sin have you had to pay a penalty for? Do you consider yourself forgiven, even though the effects of your sin remain?

12

RAHAB

Her Name Means "Storm,"
"Arrogance," "Broad," or "Spacious"

HER CHARACTER: Rahab was both clever and wise. She saw judgment coming and was able to devise an escape plan for herself and her family. As soon as she heard what God had done for the Israelites, she cast her lot with his people, risking her life in an act of faith.

KEY SCRIPTURES: Joshua 2:1–21; 6:17–25; Matthew 1:5; Hebrews 11:31; James 2:25

Then Joshua son of Nun secretly sent two spies from Shittim. "Go, look over the land," he said, "especially Jericho." So they went and entered the house of a prostitute named Rahab and stayed there. . . .

Before the spies lay down for the night, she went up on the roof and said to them, "I know that the LORD has given this land to you and that a great fear of you has fallen on us, so that all who live in this country are melting in fear because of you. . . . Now then, please swear to me by the LORD that you will show kindness to my family, because I have shown kindness to you." . . .

Then [the Israelites] burned the whole city and everything in it. . . . But Joshua spared Rahab the prostitute, with her family and all who belonged to her, because she hid the men Joshua had sent as spies to Jericho—and she lives among the Israelites to this day.

JOSHUA 2:1, 8–9, 12; 6:24–25

Rahab's Life and Times

City Walls

Jericho is probably best known today for its enormous walls, walls that fell because of the faith of the people of Israel (Hebrews 11:30). A wall around a city was its chief distinguishing mark. Anything without a wall was merely a village whose inhabitants would run to the nearest walled city for protection during a battle or war.

Rahab lived in a house on the wall of Jericho. She probably had a view not only of the city itself but also of the area outside of the protective walls. This view, which gave her the perfect vantage point for spotting potential customers as they entered and left Jericho, may have given her an advantage in running her prostitution business.

Homes, businesses, watchtowers, archer positions—all could be built on top of or within walls that were as much as twenty to thirty feet thick. The stronger the system of walls around a city (some cities had both an inner and an outer wall), the more defensible the city was against invaders who came across the plains.

Most walls of major cities were built of huge stones and mortar. Some stones of the wall of the temple in Jerusalem still exist. Their dimensions: thirty feet long, eight feet wide, and three and a half feet high. Each stone weighs an unbelievable eighty tons!

But no stone was large enough to protect the city of Jericho from the power of God through his people; no battering rams were needed to breach its walls. All that was necessary was the faith of God's people in what he said he would do. And the walls came tumbling down!

Our Life and Times

God is still in the tumbling wall business. Whatever walls in your life need breaking down—between you and a friend or family member, between you and God—God is willing to help take down.

Rahab's Legacy in Scripture

Read Joshua 2:1–18.

1. What do you think prompted Rahab to hide the Hebrew spies? Why would the house of a prostitute be a good place for the spies to go when they entered the city?

2. Although Rahab was a prostitute, the lowest profession for a woman, what good characteristics did she have?

3. Why do you think God would choose to use someone like Rahab?

4. What does this say about the people God might choose to use today to further his kingdom?

5. Rephrase in your own words Rahab's eloquent plea for her life and the lives of her family (2:9–13).

6. Why do you think the spies were willing to deal with Rahab, their lives in exchange for hers?

7. Rahab's brave actions spared not only her life but also the lives of her family members. What brave actions can you take to spare your loved ones from future difficulties and harm?

Read James 2:25.

8. James mentions Rahab in his plea for believers not to forget that works are an important outgrowth of faith. How did Rahab's actions demonstrate this truth?

9. What lessons in obedience and faith can you learn from Rahab the prostitute?

13

DEBORAH

Her Name Means "Honey Bee"

HER CHARACTER: Her vision of the world was shaped not by the political situation of her day but by her relationship with God. Though women in the ancient world did not usually become political leaders, Deborah was just the leader Israel needed—a prophetess who heard God and believed him, whose courage aroused the people, enabling them to throw off foreign oppression.

KEY SCRIPTURE: Judges 4–5

Notes

. . . *The Israelites once again did evil in the eyes of the LORD. So the LORD sold them into the hands of Jabin, a king of Canaan, who reigned in Hazor. The commander of his army was Sisera. . . . Because he had nine hundred iron chariots and had cruelly oppressed the Israelites for twenty years, they cried to the LORD for help.*

Deborah, a prophetess, the wife of Lappidoth, was leading Israel at that time. She held court under the Palm of Deborah . . . and the Israelites came to her to have their disputes decided. She sent for Barak . . . and said to him, "The LORD, the God of Israel, commands you: 'Go, take with you ten thousand men. . . . I will lure Sisera . . . and give him into your hands.'"

Barak said to [Deborah], "If you go with me, I will go; but if you don't go with me, I won't go."

"Very well," Deborah said, "I will go with you. But because of the way you are going about this, the honor will not be yours, for the LORD will hand Sisera over to a woman." So Deborah went with Barak. . . .

At Barak's advance, . . . all the troops of Sisera fell by the sword; not a man was left.

——— JUDGES 4:1–9, 15–16 ———

Deborah's Life and Times

Women as Leaders

While women leaders were uncommon in Israelite society, they were not unheard of. In this time of the judges, when Israel was spiritually malnourished, in civic disorder, and oppressed by its enemies, Deborah stepped up to the challenge. Her leadership role probably evolved gradually, as her wisdom in making judgments became known. When God spoke to Deborah, she immediately responded by calling to Barak to lead the people in a battle against their oppressor of twenty years. Barak's reluctance to go without Deborah starkly revealed Israel's lack of strong male leadership.

Deborah was the only female to hold the position of judge in Israel, but she was not the only female prophet. Several others are listed: Miriam (Exodus 15:20), Huldah (2 Kings 22:14), Noadiah (Nehemiah 6:14), Anna (Luke 2:36), and four unmarried daughters of Philip the evangelist (Acts 21:9).

Scripture describes Deborah as "a prophetess, the wife of Lappidoth." Interestingly, when Deborah described herself, she didn't use terms like prophet or wife or judge or general or leader or any other term of influence and power. She described herself as "a mother in Israel" (Judges 5:7). Her position was one of mother not only to her own biological children, but mother to all the children of Israel. Though they had forgotten not only who they were but also whom they served, their mother Deborah reminded them and led them in a victory procession to peace.

Our Life and Times

Perhaps you're not in an influential position of authority—you can still be a mother to your children and the children in your neighborhood and lead them in the right direction. Perhaps you have little power in your job or position—you can still be a mother to those around you and inspire them to righteousness. Perhaps your life allows little time or opportunity for significant positions of leadership—you can still be a mother in your sphere, whether big or small, wielding influence far beyond your lowly position. You can be like Deborah, used of God to be a mother in Israel.

Deborah's Legacy in Scripture

Read Judges 4:1–3.

1. Describe what you think conditions might have been like for a family in Israel at this time (4:1–3).

2. How do you think you would have reacted to such conditions? Like most of the Israelites? Like Deborah?

Read Judges 4:4–8.

3. What was Barak afraid of (4:8)? Why would having Deborah along alleviate those fears?

4. Which of Deborah's characteristics would you most like to have? What would you do if you had that characteristic? What can you do to develop that characteristic?

Read Judges 4:9–10.

5. How do you think the Israelite men felt about the honor for this victory going to Deborah and Jael?

6. When a woman succeeds today, what are the reactions of the men around her?

Read Judges 5:7.

7. What does Deborah call herself in this verse? What does this tell you about Deborah?

8. What lesson for your own life can you gain from this verse?

14

JAEL

Her Name Means
"A Wild or Mountain Goat"

HER CHARACTER: Decisive and courageous, she seized the opportunity to kill an enemy of God's people.

KEY SCRIPTURE: Judges 4–5

Then Deborah said to Barak, "Go! This is the day the LORD has given Sisera into your hands. . . ." So Barak went down Mount Tabor, followed by ten thousand men. At Barak's advance, the LORD routed Sisera and all his chariots and army. . . . All the troops of Sisera fell by the sword; not a man was left.

Sisera, however, fled on foot to the tent of Jael. . . .

Jael went out to meet Sisera and said to him, "Come, my lord, come right in. Don't be afraid." So he entered her tent, and she put a covering over him.

"I'm thirsty," he said. "Please give me some water." She opened a skin of milk, gave him a drink, and covered him up.

. . . Jael, Heber's wife, picked up a tent peg and a hammer and went quietly to him while he lay fast asleep, exhausted. She drove the peg through his temple into the ground, and he died.

JUDGES 4:14–19, 21

Jael's Life and Times

Bottles

When Sisera asked for a drink of water and Jael instead gave him milk, she was offering the best of the house. People of the area prized this drink, which was made by putting goat's milk into an old skin bottle and shaking it. The milk then curdled, or fermented, when mixed with the bacteria that remained in the skin bottle from a prior use.

But what on earth is a skin bottle?

Nomadic desert peoples, who were frequently on the move, found skin flasks much more useful than clay bottles, which broke easily. Women sewed goat or lamb skins together with the hairy part of the skin on the outside, then sealed them so they would hold water, milk, wine, or other liquids.

Hagar carried a skin of water into the desert with her (Genesis 21:14–15). Jael offered Sisera a drink of milk from a skin bottle (Judges 4:19). Hannah brought a skin of wine along when delivering her son Samuel to Eli the priest (1 Samuel 1:24). David carried a skin of wine to his brothers (1 Samuel 16:20). Jesus talked about not putting new wine into old, brittle wineskins (Matthew 9:17).

Our Life and Times

Christ's decree to not put new wine in old wineskins has, of course, significant meaning for us today. Are our minds and hearts like an old wineskin—brittle, hard, tough? Ready to burst when faced with new ideas or new ways of doing things? Or are our minds and hearts supple, soft, and flexible like a new skin? Are we open to learning new things about our community of believers? About ourselves? About our God?

Jael's Legacy in Scripture

Read Judges 4:14–22.

1. How did God accomplish this great victory (4:15)? Compare Judges 5:4–5.

2. God has proven over and over again that he can do what we think is impossible. What impossible things has he accomplished in your life?

3. Use three adjectives to describe Sisera. Think about the fact that he was running away from the slaughter of his men. But also think about the fact that he was the sole survivor.

4. Use three adjectives to describe Jael. Pretend you don't know what she is going to do. Pick your adjectives based only on Judges 4:17–20.

5. Which characteristics of Sisera and Jael are worth imitating? Which are worth forgetting?

6. What made Jael able to do what she did? Fear? Bravery? Desperation? How much did the more brutal culture she was a part of have to do with her actions?

Read Judges 5:24–27.

7. Why do you think Deborah praised Jael for such a savage deed?

8. What is the ultimate lesson behind the story of Deborah and Barak and Jael and all of the death woven within it?

15

DELILAH

Her Name Means "Dainty One"

HER CHARACTER: A harlot whose nationality is unknown, she used her beauty to betray her lover and enrich herself.

KEY SCRIPTURE: Judges 16:4–22

[Samson] fell in love with a woman . . . whose name was Delilah. The rulers of the Philistines went to her and said, "See if you can lure [Samson] into showing you the secret of his great strength . . . so we may . . . subdue him. Each one of us will give you eleven hundred shekels of silver."

So Delilah said to Samson, "Tell me the secret of your great strength."

. . . Then she said to him, "How can you say, 'I love you,' when you won't confide in me? This is the third time you have made a fool of me and haven't told me the secret of your great strength." With such nagging she prodded him day after day until he was tired to death.

So he told her everything. "No razor has ever been used on my head. . . ."

When Delilah saw that he had told her everything, she sent word to the rulers of the Philistines, "Come back once more; he has told me everything.". . . Having put him to sleep on her lap, she called a man to shave off the seven braids of his hair, and so began to subdue him. And his strength left him.

——— JUDGES 16:4–6, 15–19 ———

Delilah's Life and Times

H a i r

Samson's hair obviously plays a key role in the story of his rise to power and his fall from grace. He had grown it long, plaited in seven braids, because of a Nazirite vow (for more on this read Numbers 6).

Good-looking Absalom, King David's son, had so much hair that he had to cut it whenever "it became too heavy for him" (2 Samuel 14:26). Remarkably, his shorn curls weighed as much as five pounds! But Absalom's luxurious locks eventually got the better of him. During battle one day his head got caught in the branches of a large oak tree (2 Samuel 18:9). His mass of hair no doubt contributed to the entanglement. The man who had tried to wrench the kingdom from his own father swung helplessly from the tree, an easy target for his enemies.

Before being thrown to her death, Queen Jezebel not only painted her eyes but "arranged her hair" (2 Kings 9:30). The beautiful hair of the Beloved in Song of Songs is compared to a "flock of goats" and a "royal tapestry" (Song of Songs 4:1; 7:5), while the Lover's hair is described as "wavy and black as a raven" (Song of Songs 5:11). Often the Old Testament writers described living to old age—so old their hair turned gray—as a mark of God's favor and blessing (Proverbs 16:31; 20:29). People who were mourning would cut or pull out their hair in their grief (Ezra 9:3; Isaiah 22:12; Jeremiah 7:29). A sinful woman, full of anguish for her sins, poured perfume on Jesus' feet, washed them with her tears, and wiped them with her hair (Luke 7:38).

By New Testament times, men were wearing their hair shorter and only women allowed their hair to grow long. Paul was pretty adamant about this in 1 Corinthians 11:6, 14–15. Both Paul and Peter took time to warn the women of their day specifically against "braided hair," directing them to focus on inner beauty, not outward.

Our Life and Times

Women today spend millions of dollars cutting, coloring, perming, and styling their hair. But remember, no amount of money or primping can cover up a lack of inner beauty. Before arranging your hair into a becoming style, be sure to arrange your spirit into a becoming demeanor. Then you'll be beautiful outside and in.

Delilah's Legacy in Scripture

Read Judges 16:4–30.

1. Why was Delilah so willing to betray Samson? Why do you think Samson played along, giving her false answers?

2. What are Samson's strengths? What are his weaknesses?

3. What are Delilah's strengths? What are her weaknesses?

4. List five areas where you think you are strong. Now list five areas where you think you are weak. What can you do to improve in those weak areas?

5. How exactly do you think Delilah wore Samson down so that he told her the truth about his strength?

6. What does such nagging do to a relationship? If you ever nagged someone to do something, how did you feel when you finally got what you wanted?

7. How can you tell if someone is speaking the truth? How important is it to be able to discern the truth? From your children? From your husband or boyfriend? From your pastor? From politicians?

8. Not only did Samson's strength leave him, according to the end of verse 20 the Lord left him. Does it surprise you that Samson didn't realize this right away? Why or why not?

9. When have you felt at your weakest spiritually? Did you feel this way because God had left you? Or because of something you had done yourself?

10. Why do you think the story of Delilah is important? What can she teach us? Who finally wins in this story?

11. In what area of your life do you need renewed faith that good will triumph?

16

NAOMI

Her Name Means "My Joy" or "Pleasant"

HER CHARACTER: Suffering a threefold tragedy, Naomi refused to hide her sorrow or bitterness. Believing in God's sovereignty, she attributed her suffering to his will. But her fixation on circumstances, both past and present, led to hopelessness. A kind and loving mother-in-law, she inspired unusual love and loyalty in her daughters-in-law.

KEY SCRIPTURE: Ruth 1; 4:13–17

In the days when the judges ruled, there was a famine in the land, and a man from Bethlehem in Judah, together with his wife and two sons, went to live for a while in the country of Moab. The man's name was Elimelech, his wife's name Naomi, and the names of the two sons were Mahlon and Kilion. They were Ephrathites from Bethelehm, Judah. And they went to Moab and lived there.

Now Elimelech, Naomi's husband, died, and she was left with her two sons. They married Moabite women, one named Orpah and the other Ruth. After they had lived there about ten years, both Mahlon and Kilion also died, and Naomi was left without her two sons and her husband.

When she heard in Moab that the LORD had come to the aid of his people by providing food for them, Naomi and her daughters-in-law prepared to return home from there. With her two daughters-in-law she left the place where she had been living and set out on the road that would take them back to the land of Judah. . . .

Naomi said, "Return home, my daughters. Why would you come with me? Am I going to have any more sons, who could become your husbands? Return home, my daughters." . . .

At this they wept again. Then Orpah kissed her mother-in-law good-by, but Ruth clung to her. . . .

. . . So Naomi returned from Moab accompanied by Ruth the Moabitess, her daughter-in-law, arriving in Bethlehem as the barley harvest was beginning.

. . . Then Naomi took [Ruth's] child, laid him in her lap and cared for him. The women living there said, "Naomi has a son." And they named him Obed.

RUTH 1:1–7, 11–12, 14, 22; 4:16–17

Naomi's Life and Times

Famine

Pictures of the bloated stomachs and empty eyes of children dying of hunger hover in our minds long after the television is turned off. Famine today, just as in Bible times, is the great destroyer of the weak—of helpless children and defenseless elderly. The cries of mothers unable to save their hungry children echo throughout the years, a painful reminder of our dependence on the earth for our sustenance.

There are two rainy seasons in Palestine—October-November and March-April. When rain didn't fall during these two periods, famine often resulted. Famine also occurred when hail or insects destroyed the food supply or when invading armies devastated crops to bring a captured people into submission.

Throughout Scripture God uses famine to bring about his purposes. Deuteronomy 28:21–24 gives a vivid description of the famine that would come if God's people disobeyed him. Abraham and Isaac and Jacob all fled to Egypt because of famine in the land of Palestine. The events of a worldwide famine brought Joseph and then his father, Jacob, and his brothers to Egypt, where they eventually became the slaves of the pharaohs. In the book of Ruth, Naomi and her husband flee the famine in Israel, and, through their flight and its subsequent events, God brings Ruth into his holy plan as an ancestor of God's Son, Jesus.

In the New Testament, Jesus predicted that famine would be one of the signs of the end of the ages (Matthew 24:7; Mark 13:8; Luke 21:11). In the book of Acts we learn that a believer by the name of Agabus foretold a severe famine (Acts 11:28); the next verse then reveals the opportunity this gave the believers to share with each other.

In one of Scripture's most somber prophecies, Amos tells of the time when God will bring about another sort of famine: "I will send a famine through the land—not a famine of food or a thirst for water, but a famine of hearing the words of the LORD" (Amos 8:11).

In the past, God had always listened and responded when his people cried out to him, but Amos told of a time to come when their cries would be met with a frightening silence.

Our Life and Times

Who shall separate us from the love of Christ?" asks Paul. "Shall trouble or hardship or persecution or famine or nakedness or danger or sword?" (Romans 8:35). But then Paul answers his own question with that wonderful believer's cry of victory: Nothing, not even famine, will ever separate us from God's love.

Naomi's Legacy in Scripture

Read Ruth 1.

1. Describe what you think the family of Elimelech and Naomi may have been like. Keep in mind the meanings of their names: Elimelech ("my God is King"), Naomi ("pleasant"), as well as the meaning of their hometown, Bethlehem ("house of bread").

2. How is this family similar to or different from yours?

3. Choose three or four words you think would describe what Naomi experienced in verses 3–5.

4. What kind of reception do you think Naomi expected upon her return to Bethlehem with her Moabite daughters-in-law?

5. If you have ever faced a totally unclear future, what did you learn from that situation?

6. What do verses 8–18 reveal about the relationship that Naomi and Ruth had?

7. If you have a daughter-in-law, how could you be a Naomi to her?

8. Was the Lord at fault for Naomi's circumstances (1:20–21)? Was he at fault for her bitterness over them?

9. Describe one situation for which you have held or do hold bitterness.

10. What is more important in life: your circumstances or your reactions to them? Explain your answer.

17

RUTH

Her Name Means "Friendship"

HER CHARACTER: Generous, loyal, and loving, she is strong and serene, able to take unusual risks, dealing actively with the consequences.

KEY SCRIPTURES: Ruth 2–4; Matthew 1:5

And Ruth the Moabitess said to Naomi, "Let me go to the fields and pick up the leftover grain behind anyone in whose eyes I find favor."

Naomi said to her, "Go ahead, my daughter." So she went out and began to glean in the fields behind the harvesters. As it turned out, she found herself working in a field belonging to Boaz, who was from the clan of Elimelech.

. . . Then Boaz announced to the elders and all the people, "Today you are witnesses that I have bought from Naomi all the property of Elimelech, Kilion and Mahlon. I have also acquired Ruth the Moabitess, Mahlon's widow, as my wife, in order to maintain the name of the dead with his property, so that his name will not disappear from among his family or from the town records. Today you are witnesses!"

. . . So Boaz took Ruth and she became his wife. Then he went to her, and the LORD enabled her to conceive, and she gave birth to a son.

RUTH 2:2–3; 4:9–10, 13

Ruth's Life and Times

Gleaning

It was harvest time when Ruth and Naomi arrived in Bethlehem. They could not plant their own grain and harvest it. So, unless there was another way to get food, they would starve. Naomi knew the Mosaic laws and urged Ruth to follow the harvesters and "glean," or gather, what they left behind. In this way, Ruth would be able to provide food for both Naomi and herself.

The laws of Moses directed landowners to leave some of the harvest behind for the "poor and aliens." As a Moabite with no one to support her, Ruth fit both categories. Harvesters were not to reap to the very edges of their fields, nor were they to go over a field a second time to pick up what was missed the first time. This grain was to be left for the poor (Leviticus 19:9; 23:22; Deuteronomy 24:19–22). This "welfare system," set up by Moses, took care of the needy by encouraging the richer landowners to share their bounty with those less fortunate.

But it wasn't a handout. The poor still had to work for their food, following along behind the harvesters and picking up what they left behind. Depending on the efficiency of the field hands and the number of fellow gleaners reaping the grain, it could be difficult to do much more than survive. When Boaz ordered his reapers to purposely leave behind stalks of grain for Ruth to pick up, he went beyond the letter of the law.

Boaz also ordered his reapers not to "embarrass" Ruth were she to glean in the wrong part of the field, that is, if she didn't follow the rules exactly. His admonishment offers a glimpse into the heart and character of this man, who took great care to follow the Mosaic law and who, with Ruth, became an ancestor of Christ.

Our Life and Times

Was it by chance that Ruth "found herself working in a field belonging to Boaz, who was from the clan of Elimelech [Ruth's father-in-law]" (Ruth 2:3)? Of course not. Even in what appeared to be a chance situation, God was at work, divinely preparing for Ruth's and Naomi's sustenance. We make a grave mistake if we assume that what happens in our lives is merely a matter of chance or coincidence. Remember: God is at work, divinely orchestrating events to bring about his purposes in our lives.

Ruth's Legacy in Scripture

Read Ruth 2.

1. What is Ruth known for? What reputation goes with her to the field?

2. Describe what this day's work must have been like for Ruth (2:7, 17–18).

Read Ruth 3.

3. When Boaz was sleeping at the threshing floor instead of at home, was Ruth's behavior immoral? What was she asking Boaz by her behavior?

4. Through Boaz, God honored Ruth's faithfulness to Naomi and to himself. If you have been faithful through difficult circumstances, how has God shown his faithfulness to you?

Read Ruth 4.

5. Who do you think was happiest at this wedding? Ruth? Boaz? Naomi? Why? The wedding takes place in verse 13.

6. What does the outcome of this story tell you about God's providence, his divine guidance?

7. How have you experienced God's providence and his divine direction in your life?

8. After all of Ruth's sorrows, what is her situation now?

9. Naomi's restored joy is described, but nothing is said of Ruth's. In your own words, describe what sort of joy Ruth must have been experiencing.

10. Think about a time in your life when your joy was restored.

18

HANNAH

Her Name Means
"Graciousness" or "Favor"

HER CHARACTER: Provoked by another woman's malice, she refused to respond in kind. Instead, she poured out her hurt and sorrow to God, allowing him to vindicate her.

KEY SCRIPTURES: 1 Samuel 1:1–2:11; 2:19–21

Elkanah . . . had two wives; one was called Hannah and the other Peninnah. Peninnah had children, but Hannah had none. . . .

And because the LORD had closed her womb, her rival kept provoking her in order to irritate her . . . till she wept and would not eat. . . .

In bitterness of soul Hannah wept much and prayed to the LORD. And she made a vow, saying, "O LORD Almighty, if you will only look upon your servant's misery and remember me, and not forget your servant but give her a son, then I will give him to the LORD for all the days of his life." . . .

Elkanah lay with Hannah his wife, and the LORD remembered her. So in the course of time Hannah conceived and gave birth to a son. She named him Samuel, saying, "Because I asked the LORD for him."

1 SAMUEL 1:1–2, 6–7, 10–11, 19–20

Hannah's Life and Times

Infertility

Praying through her tears and so overwrought that Eli thought she was drunk, Hannah expresses for women throughout the ages the agonizing experience of infertility. The deep, unsatisfied longing for children, the pain of watching others bear one child after another, the anguish of watching a mother kiss her baby's face—Hannah experienced them all.

The Israelites saw children as a particular blessing from the Lord, recognizing his power to open or close a woman's womb. Women who couldn't bear children were considered subfemale, unable to fulfill their divine purpose on earth. When a woman was unable to fulfill this "duty," her emotional pain was tremendous. And more than likely, barren women also felt they were denied the possibility of being the one chosen to bear the Messiah.

Infertility brought with it not only a debilitating personal sorrow, but also the reproach of a woman's husband, the disapproval of a woman's family, and the rejection of society. Husbands looked to their wives to produce many sons to help in supporting the family. A woman's extended family, both her own and her husband's, looked to her to continue the family line and saw her as one who had not fulfilled her responsibility when she didn't produce children. And the social circles of young women of childbearing years by their very nature included many other young women, women who were often producing one child after another. Their fertility mocked the infertility of the barren woman every time she went to the market or to the well or to a community social event.

Scripture tells the stories of a number of women who were barren. Sarah laughed when told she would finally have a son. Rachel clutched Jacob and begged him to give her sons, as if he could open her womb. Hannah's pain made her seek help from the only One truly capable of providing it.

If Hannah had never had a child, she would still have gone down in Scripture's narrative as a woman of faith. Hannah is not a woman of faith simply because she bore a child; she is a woman of faith because she sought God when she was in her deepest distress, because she realized that only he could answer her questions and that only he could provide the consolation and purpose in life she so desperately sought.

Our Life and Times

The same is true of us. We're not considered God's faithful people because of all that happens to us. We're faithful because of how we respond to all that happens. In spite of good times or bad, God's faithful people trust him with both their present and their future.

Hannah's Legacy in Scripture

Read 1 Samuel 1.

1. What response does Hannah's childlessness cause in Hannah? in Peninnah? in Elkanah?

2. How have you responded to disappointments or failures in your life?

3. What impact did the reactions of those around you have on you?

4. Hannah stood in this very public place and poured out her pain to the Lord (1:9–14). Notice Eli's reaction. Do you think she was unaware of the reaction others might have, or do you think she just didn't care?

5. What caused the change in Hannah recorded in verse 18? Is there anything here that would make her sure she would now bear a son? If not, why then was she comforted?

6. When has God answered your prayers after a time of disappointment or difficulty? When have your prayers gone unanswered? How did God provide in those troublesome times?

7. How did God answer Hannah's prayer (1:19–20)? What is the significance of the name Samuel?

8. Verses 21–28 record Hannah's fulfillment of her vow, recorded in verse 11. What would have made Hannah's vow difficult?

Read 1 Samuel 2:18–21.

9. Describe Hannah's actions during the years when Samuel was growing up in the temple. What do you think those years were like for her?

10. How did God reward Hannah for her faithfulness?

11. Hannah dedicated her son Samuel to the Lord by giving him up to the Lord and to the work in the temple. Are your children dedicated to the Lord? If so, what are you doing to help them grow up in him?

19

MICHAL

Her Name Means
"Who Is Like God?"

HER CHARACTER: A woman of strong emotions, she was unable to control the important circumstances of her life. Forcibly separated from two husbands, she lost her father and her brother, who were savaged by their enemies.

KEY SCRIPTURES: 1 Samuel 18:20–29; 19:11–17; 2 Samuel 6:16–23

Notes

Saul's daughter Michal was in love with David. . . . "I will give her to him," [Saul] thought, "so that she may be a snare to him." . . .

When Saul realized that the LORD was with David and that his daughter Michal loved David, Saul became still more afraid of him, and he remained his enemy the rest of his days. . . .

Michal, David's wife, warned him, "If you don't run for your life tonight, tomorrow you'll be killed [by my father]." So Michal let David down through a window, and he fled and escaped. . . .

[Then] Saul [gave] his daughter Michal, David's wife, to Paltiel. . . .

Then David sent messengers to Ish-Bosheth son of Saul, demanding, "Give me my wife Michal." . . .

So Ish-Bosheth gave orders and had her taken away from her husband Paltiel son of Laish. Her husband, however, went with her, weeping behind her all the way to Bahurim. Then Abner said to him, "Go back home!" So he went back. . . .

As the ark of the LORD was entering the City of David, Michal daughter of Saul watched from a window. And when she saw King David leaping and dancing before the LORD, she despised him in her heart.

——— 1 SAMUEL 18: 20–21, 28–29; 19:11–12; 25:44; 2 SAMUEL 3:14–16; 6:16 ———

Michal's Life and Times

Worship

When David brought the ark of the covenant to Jerusalem, after it had been in Philistine hands for a number of years and after a fateful earlier attempt to move it, he did so with a deep sense of awe. The ark was moved only six steps before he stopped and sacrificed a bull and a fattened calf. Then, as the priests brought the ark into Jerusalem, David "danced before the Lord with all his might" (2 Samuel 6:14), and the people with him shouted and blew on trumpets.

David's worship of the Lord was neither subdued nor restrained. The psalms of praise he wrote also reveal his deep love for God, a love so all-encompassing it could not be contained, but burst forth in exuberant worship.

Sacrifices and offerings were an important part of worship in Old Testament times. Since sin separated the worshiper from God, sacrifice was needed to reestablish the relationship and make true worship possible. The response of praise to God took several forms: prayer, as when Solomon dedicated the temple (1 Kings 8); praise in singing as individuals (2 Samuel 23:1) and in choirs (Nehemiah 12); praise with musical instruments (Psalm 150); and praise with dancing (Exodus 15:20–21; 2 Samuel 6:14–16; Psalm 149:3).

But God makes it clear that he won't be satisfied with only the forms of worship. Sacrifices and music and dancing have no meaning apart from a heart and life truly dedicated to the Lord. God's words to the prophet Micah (6:6–8) clearly state this truth:

> With what shall I come before the Lord and bow down before the exalted God? Shall I come before him with burnt offerings, with calves a year old? Will the Lord be pleased with thousands of rams, with ten thousand rivers of oil? Shall I offer my firstborn for my transgression, the fruit of my body for the sin of my soul? He has showed you, O man, what is good. And what does the Lord require of you? To act justly and to love mercy and to walk humbly with your God.

Michal's contempt for her husband David reveals her own lack of true dedication. She was content to be a critical spectator rather than a true worshiper of God.

Our Life and Times

Whenever anyone puts appearances or tradition or form above a true desire to worship our God and Savior, we'd best step carefully . . . and read the words of God to Micah the prophet, which are as true for us today as they were for the Israelites of the prophet's day.

Michal's Legacy in Scripture

Read 1 Samuel 18:20; 19:11–17.

1. What do you think attracted Michal to David so that she fell in love with him? How far was she willing to go to protect him?

Read 1 Samuel 25:43–44; 2 Samuel 3:14.

2. How do the events in the intervening years affect Michal and her feelings for David?

Read 2 Samuel 6:12–16, 20–23.

3. Describe in your own words what you think this scene of worship looked like (6:12–15).

4. Why do you think Michal reacted as she did (6:16)? Why do you suppose she was in her room watching the scene from the window instead of in the crowd participating?

5. How often do you merely watch worship rather than participate in it? What needs to happen in order for you to become a participant instead of a spectator?

6. How often are you more concerned with appearances than you should be? Why? What can you do to change?

7. What is David trying to tell Michal in verses 21–22? Do you think Michal had any idea of the depth of love David had for God? Why or why not?

8. How hard would it be for you to claim verse 22, as David does here? Do you think God wants this sort of submissiveness from everyone? Why or why not?

20

ABIGAIL

Her Name Means
"My Father Is Joy"

HER CHARACTER: Generous, quick-witted, and wise, she is one of the Bible's great peacemakers.

KEY SCRIPTURE: 1 Samuel 25:2–42

A certain man . . . was very wealthy. . . . His name was Nabal and his wife's name was Abigail. She was an intelligent and beautiful woman, but . . . [Nabal] was surly and mean in his dealings. . . .

One of the servants told Nabal's wife Abigail: "David sent messengers from the desert to give our master his greetings, but he hurled insults at them. . . . Disaster is hanging over our . . . whole household."

Abigail lost no time. . . .

As she came riding her donkey into a mountain ravine, there were David and his men. . . .

When Abigail saw David, she quickly . . . fell at his feet and said: "My lord, let the blame be on me alone. . . . Pay no attention to that wicked man Nabal. He is just like his name—his name is Fool. . . ."

David said to Abigail, "Praise be to the LORD, the God of Israel, who has sent you today to meet me. May you be blessed for your good judgment and for keeping me from bloodshed this day." . . .

About ten days later, the LORD struck Nabal and he died.

When David heard that Nabal was dead, he . . . sent word to Abigail, asking her to become his wife.

1 SAMUEL 25:2–3, 14, 17–18, 20, 23–25, 32–33, 38–39

Abigail's Life and Times

Food

Two hundred loaves of bread, two skins of wine, five dressed sheep, a bushel of roasted grain, a hundred cakes of raisins, and two hundred cakes of pressed figs—what a feast! Abigail put together a marvelous meal for David and his men.

Even though famine was not unknown in the area, Palestine had the reputation of being a "land of milk and honey." The most basic food of the land was bread. The bread of biblical times was coarse, dark, and rich. Field workers often brought two small hollow loaves of bread with them, one filled with olives and the other with cheese. Abigail's offering of two hundred loaves of such bread formed a bountiful beginning to the meal for David and his men.

Wine was the common drink in this hot land. Juices fermented quickly in bags of animal skins. Often wine was mixed with water to provide a refreshing drink with meals. Wine also found use as a disinfectant (Luke 10:34) and as a medicine (1 Timothy 5:23).

Next Abigail took five "dressed sheep." No, this didn't mean the sheep wore clothes appropriate for the trip; it meant they were killed and skinned and ready to be cooked. Because the sheep were dressed, David's men merely had to build a fire and cook parts of the sheep to eat. Sheep, both young and old, formed a major part of the Israelites' meat diet, as did calves, goats, and different types of birds. Hunters also brought in venison, antelope, and other wild animals, and fishermen provided many types of fish for eating, something the Israelites complained about missing while they were wandering in the desert.

The bushel of roasted grain was a food that could be eaten anywhere, anytime. Since David and his men were often pursued, such food would have been a helpful addition to their diet. Such roasted grain along with a bit of wine often formed a quick lunch for field laborers (Ruth 2:14).

Now for dessert—or at least something sweet. Abigail gathered one hundred cakes of raisins and two hundred cakes of pressed figs. Palestine swelled with the produce from the vine and fig tree, so much so that the tree came to be known as a metaphor for safe, abundant living: "During Solomon's lifetime Judah and Israel, from Dan to Beersheba, lived in safety, each man under his own vine and fig tree" (1 Kings 4:25). Fresh fruit of many different kinds was available year round, but the first fresh figs of the year were considered a special delicacy. Dried figs and raisins also made excellent food for the traveler, perfect for David and his men.

The females in Israelite households (some things never change!) customarily prepared the meals. They usually prepared food in a mixed form; that is, small pieces of meat, vegetables, rice, grain, and sometimes fruits were mixed together to form the meal rather than being kept separate. The Israelite diet could be almost as varied—depending on the season and the individual's wealth—as many of today's people have come to expect and enjoy.

Our Life and Times

New Testament writers used food as a metaphor for spiritual nourishment. Paul talks about the milk rather than solid food required by us when we are new Christians (1 Corinthians 3:2), and the writer to the Hebrews writes of those Christians whose spiritual growth is so slow that they still require milk rather than solid food (Hebrews 5:11–14). Jesus reminded us and his disciples that "life is more than food" (Luke 12:23–26), and that we shouldn't worry so much about it.

Abigail's Legacy in Scripture

Read 1 Samuel 25:1–13.

1. How does this description of Nabal and Abigail (25:3) set the stage for what is to come?

2. These verses reveal what a mismatched couple Nabal and Abigail were. How do women in Abigail's position cope?

3. Compare the words of David (25:6–8) with the words of Nabal (25:10–11). What does that tell you about each man?

4. What do the words of those around you tell you about who they are and what they are like? What do your words reveal about you?

5. Why was David's reaction (25:13) the wrong reaction?

6. What does Luke 6:27–31 have to say about how you should react when you've been wronged?

Read 1 Samuel 25:14–42.

7. What do verses 14–17 tell you about Abigail's relationship with the servants in the household? What did the servants think of their master, Nabal?

8. Are you more like an Abigail or more like a Nabal to those who are in your care? Your coworkers? Your children? Your husband? Your extended family?

9. How do you react when someone in authority makes a bad choice? If the choice affects you, what should you do?

10. Compare David and Nabal's actions. How often do you respond like David? Like Nabal?

11. Why do you think David was so quick to ask Abigail to marry him (25:40)? Was he attracted to her? Did he feel responsible for her? Did he admire her?

12. What Davids do you have in your life? What Nabals? What can you learn from Abigail about living and working with each of these men?

21

THE WOMAN OF ENDOR

HER CHARACTER: Compassionate to Saul on the eve of his death, she exercised power by acting as a medium.

KEY SCRIPTURE: 1 Samuel 28:3–25

꙳

Now Samuel was dead, and . . . Saul had expelled the mediums and spiritists from the land.

The Philistines . . . set up camp at Shunem, while Saul gathered all the Israelites and set up camp at Gilboa. When Saul saw the Philistine army . . . terror filled his heart. He inquired of the LORD, but the LORD did not answer him. . . . Saul then said to his attendants, "Find me a woman who is a medium, so I may go and inquire of her."

"There is one in Endor," they said.

So Saul disguised himself, putting on other clothes, and at night he and two men went to the woman. "Consult a spirit for me," he said, "and bring up for me the one I name."

. . . Then the woman asked, "Whom shall I bring up for you?"

"Bring up Samuel," he said. . . .

"An old man wearing a robe is coming up," she said.

Then Saul knew it was Samuel, and he bowed down and . . . said, "The Philistines are fighting against me, and God has turned away from me. . . . So I have called on you to tell me what to do."

Samuel said . . . "The LORD will hand over both Israel and you to the Philistines."

1 SAMUEL 28:3–8, 11, 14–16, 19

The Woman of Endor's Life and Times

Witchcraft

Ironic, isn't it, that the same Saul who refused to heed Samuel's prophetic words when he was alive now disobeyed the very laws he had put into effect in order to hear from Samuel one last time. Saul's desperation must have been very great for him to consult with a medium, to dabble in the occult.

Ancient peoples felt as though they were living in close contact with the spirit world around them. They depended on divination—foretelling of the future—to help them avoid possible troubles ahead, and used occult rituals to attempt to gain control over people, objects, and even nature.

Magicians studied the entrails of animals and the flights of birds to discover information about the future. They examined the stars and interpreted dreams. They called on the dead to make use of their wisdom. At times, they even gathered information from such common occurrences as a sneeze.

Right from the start, God commanded his people not to have anything to do with witchcraft in any form. His words are clear and firm—we might even think harsh: "A man or woman who is a medium or spiritist among you must be put to death. You are to stone them; their blood will be on their own heads" (Leviticus 20:27).

Our Life and Times

Today, when the interest in spiritism and mediums is once again strong, it is good to consider what may be fueling the fascination. Words like *waiting*, *depending*, *surrendering*, and *obeying* rankle. We would much rather find ways to control the course of events. Yet the spiritual life is often counterintuitive. When we embrace the way of faith and trust in God, following him even when the path is unfamiliar or unknown, what seems like it should diminish us actually enlarges us. The story of Saul and the woman of Endor remind us that there's really nothing new about human behavior. Under the skin we all experience the same desires, temptations, and needs. Then, as now, our happiness lies in faith and trust.

The Woman of Endor's Legacy in Scripture

Read 1 Samuel 28.

1. The woman of Endor enters this story fearfully. Why was she afraid? Why did she think meeting with Saul might bring about her death?

2. Who do you think appears? Is it really Samuel, or is it another spirit impersonating Samuel? What does this tell you about occult practices?

3. What "spirits" have you consulted in order to know or plan your future, or just for "fun"? Horoscopes? Cards? Fortune-tellers? Ouija boards? How do you react when told nothing like this should ever be done just for "fun"?

4. How did Saul react when he found out he would die the next day (28:19)?

5. How would you react if you truly knew today was your last day alive? What would you do?

6. What does the woman of Endor's reaction to Saul in these verses tell you about her underlying character?

7. When have you shown kindness to someone you knew for sure was in the wrong? What did you do?

22

BATHSHEBA

Her Name Means "The Seventh Daughter"
or "The Daughter of an Oath"

HER CHARACTER: Her beauty made her a victim of a king's desire. Though it is difficult to discern her true character, she seems to have found the courage to endure tragedy, winning the king's confidence and eventually securing the kingdom for her son Solomon.

KEY SCRIPTURE: 2 Samuel 11:1–12:25

ン

One evening David got up from his bed and walked around on the roof of the palace. From the roof he saw a woman bathing. The woman was very beautiful. . . . Then David sent messengers to get her. She came to him, and he slept with her. . . . The woman conceived and sent word to David, saying, "I am pregnant."

. . . In the morning David wrote a letter to Joab . . . "Put Uriah [Bathsheba's husband] in the front line where the fighting is fiercest. Then withdraw from him so he will be struck down and die." . . .

When Uriah's wife heard that her husband was dead, she mourned for him. After the time of mourning was over, David had her brought to his house, and she became his wife and bore him a son. But the thing David had done displeased the LORD.

2 SAMUEL 11:2, 4–5, 14–15, 26–27

Bathsheba's Life and Times

Ritual Bathing

A warm tub of water with a fragrance of flowers, soaking, eyes closed. That's the image conjured up in most of our minds when it comes to bathing. But in Bathsheba's day, most bathing took place not for the purpose of physical cleanliness—people of that time had little knowledge of the spread of disease and germs through uncleanness. Most bathing took place to become ritually clean after a period of being unclean.

Bathsheba had just completed her monthly period. The flow of blood was finished; the seven days prescribed in Leviticus 15:19 were past, and she now needed to cleanse herself. She probably stood in or near a basin of water, using a sponge or cloth to clean herself, then either squeezing water over herself as a rinse or pouring water from a pitcher over her body.

Scripture mentions cleansing with water hundreds of times, most of them referring to ritual rather than physical cleansing. Cleansing took place after many kinds of skin diseases were healed (Leviticus 14:8), and after men and women had unusual discharges (Leviticus 15:13). Men and women both had to wash themselves after sexual intercourse to be ceremonially clean (Leviticus 15:18). Priests cleansed themselves before offering sacrifices (Exodus 29:4; Leviticus 8:6), and the sacrifices themselves were washed before being offered to God (Leviticus 1:9).

Physical cleansing more often took the form of washing one's hands before eating or washing one's feet when entering a house. Dirty, dusty roads and open sandals made foot washing something that needed to be done frequently. Since foot washing was commonly the job of the lowest member or servant of a household, Jesus modeled a splendid humility when he bathed his disciples' feet in the Upper Room (John 13:5).

The Bible sometimes describes the righteous as those with "clean hands" (Job 17:9; Psalm 24:4). Cleanliness is also used in Scripture as a metaphor for being forgiven: "I am clean and free from guilt" (Job 33:9). "Cleanse me with hyssop, and I will be clean; wash me, and I will be whiter than snow" (Psalm 51:7). In the end times, the bride of Christ will be dressed in "fine linen, bright and clean" (Revelation 19:8).

Our Life and Times

We live in a culture that glorifies outward cleanliness with our soaps and lotions and toothpastes and disinfectants, our bathing and brushing, or washing and wiping. But how concerned are we with inner cleanliness? Do we have clean hands but spirits filthy with hate? Do we have soft, clean-shaven legs but hearts hardened to the hurts of others? Do we have clean, blemish-free faces that seldom smile? Outward cleanliness is admirable—but only if an inward cleanliness accompanies it.

Bathsheba's Legacy in Scripture

Read 2 Samuel 11:2–5.

1. What might Bathsheba have been thinking when David's men came to get her? Could she have said no to David the king?

2. What part do you think Bathsheba played in the events outlined in these verses? Totally innocent? Artful seductress? Or something in between?

3. How do you resist your most frequent temptation? What path away from temptation could David and Bathsheba have taken?

4. Describe how you think Bathsheba probably felt when she realized she was pregnant with David's child. Why did she immediately tell David?

5. What would you have done in Bathsheba's situation? What would your primary feeling have been? Fear? Guilt? Joy at being pregnant? Anger at David?

Read 2 Samuel 11:6–27; 12:13.

6. These verses outline in frightening detail the depth to which David would go to cover up his sin with Bathsheba. How could God possibly say that David was a "man after my own heart" (Acts 13:22)?

7. What makes us acceptable in God's eyes: the fact that we're sinless, or the fact that we're repentant and forgiven? How does this change how you feel before God?

Read 2 Samuel 12:1–23.

8. What character represents Bathsheba in Nathan the prophet's story? What does that tell you about what God thought of her part in these events?

9. Describe a time when you were the innocent victim. How did you "pick up the pieces" even though you weren't at fault?

10. Verses 15–23 recount David's reaction to the sickness and death of his son. Where was Bathsheba during this time? What was she likely experiencing?

Read 2 Samuel 12:24–25.

11. Bathsheba now accepts comfort from David (12:24), the very man who had brought all this misery on her. Does that surprise you? Why or why not?

12. Solomon's name from the Lord was actually Jedidiah, which means "loved by the Lord." What sense of God's restoration for Bathsheba and David does this name give you?

23

TAMAR, DAUGHTER OF KING DAVID

Her Name Means "Date Tree" or "Palm Tree"

Notes

HER CHARACTER: Tamar shared her father David's good looks. Young and innocent, she was naive to the danger that threatened from her own family.

KEY SCRIPTURE: 2 Samuel 13:1–22

Ↄ

Amnon son of David fell in love with Tamar, the beautiful sister of Absalom son of David.

Amnon became frustrated to the point of illness on account of his sister Tamar, for she was a virgin, and it seemed impossible for him to do anything to her.

. . . Amnon lay down and pretended to be ill. When the king came to see him, Amnon said to him, "I would like my sister Tamar to come and make some special bread in my sight, so I may eat from her hand."

David sent word to Tamar at the palace: "Go to the house of your brother Amnon and prepare some food for him." So Tamar went to the house of her brother Amnon, who was lying down. She took some dough, kneaded it, made the bread in his sight and baked it. Then she took the pan and served him the bread, but he refused to eat.

"Send everyone out of here," Amnon said. So everyone left him. Then Amnon said to Tamar, "Bring the food here into my bedroom so I may eat from your hand." And Tamar took the bread she had prepared and brought it to her brother Amnon in his bedroom. But when she took it to him to eat, he grabbed her and said, "Come to bed with me, my sister."

"Don't, my brother!" she said to him. "Don't force me. . . . Don't do this wicked thing. . . ." But he refused to listen to her, and since he was stronger than she, he raped her.

Then Amnon hated her with intense hatred. In fact, he hated her more than he had loved her. Amnon said to her, "Get up and get out!"

. . . Tamar put ashes on her head and tore the ornamented robe she was wearing. She put her hand on her head and went away, weeping aloud as she went.

. . . And Tamar lived in her brother Absalom's house, a desolate woman.

1 SAMUEL 13:1–2, 6–12, 14–15, 19–20

Tamar's Life and Times

R a p e

Tamar's half brother, Amnon, raped her. These stark words don't begin to communicate the humiliation and despair that raped women experience. This account in 2 Samuel 13 movingly describes Tamar's pleas to her brother not to do this to her, pleas that echo through hundreds of years of women who have been forced into the sexual act against their will. "Since he was stronger," Amnon could force himself on her, and Tamar had no effective means of resistance.

God's reaction to sexual sin is evident throughout the Bible. He doesn't turn away from the victim, and he doesn't allow the rapist to go unpunished. Deuteronomy 22:25 says that "the man who has done this shall die." Leviticus 18:29 reminds the Israelites that "everyone who does any of these detestable things—such persons must be cut off from their people." In the New Testament, Paul repeatedly reminds believers to pursue sexual purity: "Let us behave decently, as in the daytime, not in orgies and drunkenness, not in sexual immorality and debauchery, not in dissension and jealousy. Rather, clothe yourselves with the Lord Jesus Christ" (Romans 13:13–14). "Flee from sexual immorality" (1 Corinthians 6:18). "Among you there must not be even a hint of sexual immorality" (Ephesians 5:3).

Amnon went unpunished by his father but died when Tamar's brother Absalom took his revenge—he didn't go unpunished forever. And what about Tamar, the beautiful virgin princess in her rich royal robes? She felt too degraded to go back to her own home in David's palace. How could she face her other virgin sisters? Instead, she went to live as "a desolate woman" with her brother Absalom. The effects of rape on its victims is the same today: desolation, grief, misery.

Our Life and Times

The Bible doesn't gloss over the fact that God's people participated in these dreadful acts; it describes many instances of rape, incest, homosexuality, and adultery. Why would a holy God think it necessary to include such sordid stories in Scripture? Perhaps because he knows our thoughts and actions, even if the world is blind to them. Through these stories God reminds us that he never forsakes his own, whether victim or criminal. Just as he offers help and comfort to the victims, never forsaking them in their trouble, he also offers healing and forgiveness to the evildoer who seeks him.

Tamar's Legacy in Scripture

Read 2 Samuel 13:1–20.

1. What does Amnon's willingness to use deceit tell you about his "love" for Tamar?

2. When have you used deceit to get your own way? How did the situation turn out? Was it worth it?

3. Why do you think David was willing to allow Tamar to nurse Amnon (13:7)? Do you think he was aware of any danger?

4. Read verses 8–10 carefully and note Tamar's actions. What do they tell you about her? Did she trust Amnon? Describe a time when you have been hurt by someone you trusted.

5. Describe your feelings as a woman when you read Tamar's pleas (13:12–13).

6. Why do you think Amnon's feelings changed so quickly (13:15)?

7. This story is an extreme case of someone who used another person to satisfy his or her own needs. In less drastic ways, how do we use other people as if they were objects to satisfy our own needs? Why is this wrong? What is our best response if we're the one being used?

8. What could Tamar possibly have meant by "sending me away" being a "greater wrong" than rape (13:16)? What did she want from Amnon?

9. Why do you think Tamar went to live in Absalom's house? Compare her future before and after the rape.

10. What has happened to you in the past that dramatically affected the way your life turned out? Was it a change for good? For bad? How has God used that circumstance to bring about his work in your life?

Read 2 Samuel 13:21–29.

11. What was father David's reaction to what had happened between his son and his daughter (13:21)? What should he have done to Amnon? What could he have done for Tamar?

12. How long did Absalom wait to get his revenge on Amnon? What effect do you think Absalom's actions have on him? On David? On Tamar?

13. When you've been hurt, have you gotten the support you needed from your family? If not, where did you go for help?

24

THE WISE WOMAN OF ABEL BETH MAACAH

HER CHARACTER: Rather than passively waiting for someone else to save her city, she had the wisdom and courage to act quickly and decisively.

KEY SCRIPTURE: 2 Samuel 20:14–22

〲

All the men of Israel deserted David to follow Sheba son of Bicri. But the men of Judah stayed by their king. . . .

David said to Abishai, ". . . Take your master's men and pursue him, or he will find fortified cities and escape from us." So . . . all the mighty warriors went out under the command of Abishai. They marched out from Jerusalem to pursue Sheba son of Bicri.

. . . Sheba passed through all the tribes of Israel to Abel Beth Maacah. . . . All the troops with Joab came and besieged Sheba in Abel Beth Maacah. They built a siege ramp up to the city, and it stood against the outer fortifications. While they were battering the wall to bring it down, a wise woman called from the city, "Listen! Listen! . . . Are you Joab?"

"I am," he answered.

. . . She continued, ". . . We are the peaceful and faithful in Israel. You are trying to destroy a city that is a mother in Israel. . . ."

Joab replied, ". . . That is not the case. A man named Sheba son of Bicri, from the hill country of Ephraim, has lifted up his hand against the king, against David. Hand over this one man, and I'll withdraw from the city."

The woman said to Joab, "His head will be thrown to you from the wall."

Then the woman went to all the people with her wise advice, and they cut off the head of Sheba son of Bicri and threw it to Joab. So he sounded the trumpet, and his men dispersed from the city, each returning to his home.

2 SAMUEL 20:2, 6–7, 14–22

The Wise Woman's Life and Times

Siege

When Joab's men gathered outside of Abel Beth Maacah, a wise woman braved the warriors gathered outside and bargained with Joab for the life of Abel's inhabitants. No doubt she and others like her were part of the reason that Abel was known as "a city that is a mother in Israel" (2 Samuel 20:19), a place to go for answers to life's difficult questions. Its inhabitants must have been shrewd as well as wise to gain such notoriety.

War was a regular feature of life for the Israelites, so much so that freedom from war gained special notice in Scripture (Joshua 11:23; 14:15; 2 Chronicles 14:6–7). Battles between opposing armies were often waged in valleys or other wide-open spaces. Inhabitants of embattled areas would flee to the nearest walled and fortified city. To gain entrance and control of such a city, armies would gather outside the city walls and prevent anyone from going in or going out. When water and food became scarce or ran out altogether, the city's inhabitants would be forced to surrender.

When a city surrendered, its populace could look forward to one of two consequences: death or slavery. Often the deprivation and horror of a siege were preferable to surrender. Depending on how well the city was prepared, a siege could last anywhere from days to weeks to months. An army of Egypt besieged the city of Ashdod for an incredible twenty-nine years, the longest siege recorded in the Bible.

Occupants of fortified cities spent much time in preparation for sieges. They strengthened the walls, gathered and stored extra food, and figured out a way to gather and store large amounts of water. Some cities built long underground tunnels to allow water to flow freely into the city. Builders of these tunnels took care to disguise the water's source, for armies could then easily cut it off or use it to gain entrance into the city. Sometimes huge cisterns were dug within the city walls to catch and store rain water.

The attacking army outside a city's walls would move vast amounts of earth to build ramps to the upper parts of the city wall. From these ramps they would then use battering rams to attempt to break down the wall in that area, all the while defending themselves against the arrows and rocks and darts of the city's inhabitants.

Joab's army built such a ramp and battered the wall of Abel in order to capture it and the rebel Sheba who had taken refuge within. But rather than throwing down arrows or rocks, the wise woman of Abel shouted words of conciliation, and in so doing, preserved innocent lives.

The Wise Woman's Legacy in Scripture

Read 2 Samuel 20:15–19.

1. In your own words, describe what you think it might have been like for a mother with several small children within the city walls of Abel.

2. While it is unlikely that you or your family have ever been in this situation, many households today are held captive by abuse, financial misfortune, grief, or illness—whether physical or mental. Do you know someone in such a situation? A child? Another woman? A teen? What can you do to help?

3. What do Joab's terse words reveal about his reaction to this brave woman (20:17)?

4. Have you ever been in a situation where the wise thing to do also required bravery? Did you do it? Why or why not?

5. What might have given the town of Abel the reputation described here? What does this tell you about its inhabitants?

6. Where do you go when you need answers?

Read 2 Samuel 20:20–22.

7. What is your reaction to what the town of Abel did with Sheba? Do you think the bargain they struck with Joab was a good one? Why or why not?

8. The facts of this story are physically brutal and disturbing, but the facts of life for many today in our society are just as brutal. How can you be a wise woman in your corner of the world?

25

RIZPAH

Her Name Means
"A Hot Stone or Coal"

HER CHARACTER: Saul's concubine Rizpah was the mother of Armoni
and Mephibosheth. Though a woman with few rights
and little power, she displayed great courage and loyalty after the death of her sons.

KEY SCRIPTURE: 2 Samuel 21:8–14

༯

   [David] the king took . . . the two sons of . . . Rizpah, whom she had
borne to Saul, together with the five sons of Saul's daughter Merab. . . . He
handed them over to the Gibeonites, who killed and exposed them on a hill
before the LORD.
   . . . Rizpah daughter of Aiah took sackcloth and spread it out for herself
on a rock. From the beginning of the harvest till the rain poured down from
the heavens on the bodies, she did not let the birds of the air touch them by
day or the wild animals by night. When David was told what Aiah's daugh-
ter Rizpah, Saul's concubine, had done, he went and took the bones of Saul
and his son Jonathan from the citizens of Jabesh Gilead. . . . David brought
the bones of Saul and his son Jonathan from there, and the bones of those
who had been killed and exposed were gathered up.
   They buried the bones of Saul and his son Jonathan in the tomb of
Saul's father Kish, at Zela in Benjamin.

——— 2 SAMUEL 21:8–14 ———

Rizpah's Life and Times

Burial and Mourning

After her sons were killed and their bodies flung on a hill, Rizpah kept a lonely vigil, warding off the birds that would peck at their flesh and the animals that would try to drag their bodies away. To allow these grown sons to be ravaged by the animals in the area was unthinkable to Rizpah.

Burial in biblical times was an occasion for showing love and respect for someone who had died. Loved ones usually buried the dead the same day as the death took place, or at least within twenty-four hours (John 11:17, 39). Family members washed the body, anointed it with herbs and spices, then wrapped it in a cloth (John 11:44). The burial itself frequently took place in a cave or in a tomb hewn from the rock so prevalent in Palestine. The same cave or tomb would be used by many members of one family (Genesis 49:29–32).

Official mourning for the dead began with the playing of the flute as soon as the death took place. These mournful flute players not only played throughout the preparation for the burial, they also accompanied the procession to the place of burial and continued to play during the official time of mourning, usually seven days (Matthew 9:23). Professional mourners were often also present, accompanying the family to the grave site and staying with the family afterward, adding to the family's customary tears, wailing, and crying (Jeremiah 9:17).

Our Life and Times

Jesus wept at the burial site of his friend Lazarus (John 11:1–43). In his human nature, Jesus understood the finality of death for those who went on living. He participated in the customs of the day and wept with Lazarus's friends and family. But in his divine nature, Jesus also understood the transitory nature of life and the fact that death is not an appalling conclusion but a glorious beginning.

Rizpah's Legacy in Scripture

Read 2 Samuel 21:7–14.

1. Why wasn't Jonathan's son Mephibosheth executed at this time too?

2. This killing pretty much annihilated Saul's descendants. Why would David order such wholesale executions?

3. Rizpah's vigil probably lasted several months. How difficult do you think it was? What drove her on?

4. Have you ever undertaken a task that, had you known what was required, would have seemed beyond your ability or strength? What kept you going? What was the result?

5. What do you think induced David to gather up these bones and bury them? His own sense of what was right? Pity for Rizpah? Respect for the dead?

6. When have you had to have some outside circumstance stimulate you to do what was right? What was the outcome? What would have happened had you done nothing?

7. How is God's love for you like Rizpah's love for her children?

26

THE QUEEN
OF SHEBA

Notes

HER CHARACTER: Though a pagan queen like Jezebel, she prized wisdom above power. She appears to have been intellectually gifted, with a good head for business and diplomacy.

KEY SCRIPTURES: 1 Kings 10:1–13; Matthew 12:42

᙮

When the queen of Sheba heard about the fame of Solomon and his relation to the name of the LORD, she came to test him with hard questions. Arriving at Jerusalem with a very great caravan—with camels carrying spices, large quantities of gold, and precious stones—she came to Solomon and talked with him about all that she had on her mind. Solomon answered all her questions; nothing was too hard for the king to explain to her. . . .

She said to the king, "The report I heard in my own country about your achievements and your wisdom is true. But I did not believe these things until I came and saw with my own eyes. Indeed, not even half was told me; in wisdom and wealth you have far exceeded the report I heard. . . . Praise be to the LORD your God, who has delighted in you and placed you on the throne of Israel."

1 KINGS 10:1–3, 6–7, 9

The Queen of Sheba's Life and Times

Gift Giving

Four-and-a-half tons of gold. And that was just part of the gift the Queen of Sheba gave to Solomon when she visited him in Jerusalem. She had probably heard of his riches as well as his wisdom and knew that no puny gift would do; something magnificent was in order. Imagine a caravan of camel after camel entering Jerusalem, bearing gifts for Solomon. A camel could carry about two hundred pounds when traveling through the desert (a staggering four hundred pounds plus its rider on shorter, less strenuous journeys). That means forty-five camels were required to carry just the gold!

Most personal meetings in ancient cultures included gift giving. A visit to someone's home required bringing along a gift for the host or hostess. Even chance encounters in the desert included gift exchanges (Genesis 14:18–20). Gift giving in ancient cultures was also a way of expressing submission to someone who was in a superior position, whether in government, in the military, or in religious life. At times, a gift might be given to gain favor or even to bribe someone in a superior position.

Some of the gifts mentioned in the Old Testament are pretty staggering in scope. Check out the gifts of gold, silver, and clothing that Abraham's servant gave to Rebekah and her family (Genesis 24:53). These gifts—the bride price, or the dowry—given by the groom's family to the bride's family formed a significant part of the traditions surrounding marriage. One of Solomon's wives received an entire town from her father as a wedding gift (1 Kings 9:16). Jacob's reconciliation gift to Esau consisted of a herd of 550 animals (Genesis 32:13–15). Besides the thousands of animals the Israelites gave as a gift to God after their victory over the Midianites, they gave gold and silver jewelry, which weighed a total of 420 pounds (Numbers 31:51–52).

The Queen of Sheba wasn't the only one who brought gifts to Solomon; so many brought gifts of "silver and gold, robes, weapons and spices, and horses and mules" that in Solomon's time silver was "as common in Jerusalem as stones" (1 Kings 10:23–27). Probably some of the most famous gifts in the Bible were those given by the Magi to the child Jesus (Matthew 2:11).

The New Testament writers often talked about the gifts we give not to each other but to God. No gift, no matter how small, is displeasing to God if it is given with a generous and cheerful heart. In fact, Jesus praised the widow who gave only two small coins because she gave all she had

Notes

out of a heart of love for God, contrasting her with the others who gave a small amount of their wealth, often grudgingly (Luke 21:1–4). More important to God than the size of our gifts is the condition of our hearts when we give (2 Corinthians 9:7).

Our Life and Times

But greater and finer and more thrilling than any gift we can give to each other or to God are the gifts he gives to us. Solomon, in the midst of all his wealth and wisdom, thanked God for the gift of a good and simple life: satisfying work to do, peaceful rest at night, a bit of happiness (Ecclesiastes 3:13; 5:19). Matthew quotes Jesus telling his followers of God's wonderful care of us and his willingness to give us good things: "If you, then, though you are evil, know how to give good gifts to your children, how much more will your Father in heaven give good gifts to those who ask him!" (Matthew 7:11). But the crowning touch, the gift worth more than all the gold in the world, is the gift God so lovingly and willingly gave us of eternal life through his Son (Romans 6:23). No thank-you note is required, just a life of gratitude to God. In the words of Paul, "Thanks be to God for his indescribable gift!" (2 Corinthians 9:15).

The Queen of Sheba's Legacy in Scripture

Read 1 Kings 10:1–5, 10.

1. What two things did the Queen of Sheba know about Solomon?

2. Think of one famous person. What made that person famous? If you could meet one famous person, who would that person be? What person can you think of who is famous because of "his relation to the name of the Lord"?

3. What does the Queen of Sheba's gift to Solomon (10:2, 10) tell you about her nation's wealth? Why would she bring such extravagant gifts?

4. What's the most extravagant gift you've ever given to another person? To God?

5. What's easier for you to give: a gift you can buy or a gift that requires that you give something of yourself?

6. What questions do you think the Queen of Sheba asked of Solomon (10:2–3)?

7. If you could have an audience with Solomon, what one question would you ask him?

8. What two things about Solomon most impressed the Queen of Sheba (10:4–5)?

9. Do you know anyone whom you think is truly wise? What impresses you most about that person?

Read 1 Kings 10:6–9, 13.

10. From everything you've read about the Queen of Sheba here, how would you describe her?

11. Is there anything in her character that you wish were true of you? What can you do to develop yourself in that area?

27

JEZEBEL

Her Name Means "Where Is the Prince (Baal)?"
or "The Prince (Baal) Exists"

HER CHARACTER: A religious woman, she spread idolatry throughout
Israel. Powerful, cunning, and arrogant, she actively
opposed God, even in the face of indisputable proofs
of his sovereignty.

Notes

KEY SCRIPTURES: 1 Kings 16:29–33; 18:1–19:2; 21:1–25; 2 Kings 9

꘡

*Ahab son of Omri did more evil in the eyes of the LORD than any of
those before him. . . . [H]e also married Jezebel . . . and began to serve Baal
and worship him.*

. . . Jezebel was killing off the LORD's prophets. . . .

*Now Ahab told Jezebel everything Elijah had done and how he had
killed all the prophets [of Baal] with the sword [on Mount Carmel]. So
Jezebel sent a messenger to Elijah to say, "May the gods deal with me, be it
ever so severely, if by this time tomorrow I do not make your life like that of
one of them."*

*. . . (There was never a man like Ahab, who sold himself to do evil in
the eyes of the LORD, urged on by Jezebel his wife.)*

*. . . Then the prophet [Elisha] poured the oil on Jehu's head and
declared, "This is what the LORD, the God of Israel, says: 'I anoint you
king over the LORD's people Israel. You are to destroy the house of Ahab
your master, and I will avenge the blood of my servants the prophets and the
blood of all the LORD's servants shed by Jezebel. . . . Dogs will devour her
on the plot of ground at Jezreel, and no one will bury her.'"*

——— 1 KINGS 16:30–31; 18:4; 19:1–2; 21:25; 2 KINGS 9:6–7, 10 ———

Jezebel's Life and Times

Baal Worship

Jezebel. Her name is synonymous with wickedness. Of all the beautiful biblical names used for children today, you won't find one Jezebel.

The daughter of Ethbaal, king of Sidon, Jezebel was raised and trained in Baal worship. She spent the years of her reign not only worshiping Baal but forcing Baal worship on her subjects. Statues of Baal showed him standing straight and tall wearing a helmet topped with bull's horns, a sign of power and fertility. In one hand he held a spear entwined with leaves, possibly symbolizing lightning and plant growth. His other hand held a club, which may have symbolized strength or thunder.

Baal worship involved the use of incense and sacrifice so common in the forms of worship of that day. The sacrifice at times involved innocent humans (Jeremiah 19:5). Also, since the main function of the god Baal was to make the land and animals and people fertile, fertility rites formed the chief part of Baal worship. Male and female attendants performed sexual acts in order to induce Baal to lavish fertility on the land.

The worship of Baal held a unique attraction for the people of Israel. When they wandered from their faith in the one true God, they often wandered toward trust in the false god Baal. The Israelites worshiped Baal during the time of Barak and Balaam (Numbers 22:41), as well as during the time of the judges (Judges 2:13; 6:28–32). Even after Elijah's triumph over Baal on Mount Carmel and the death of 850 priests of Baal that day, Baal worship continued off and on all during the reigns of the kings of Israel and Judah.

Our Life and Times

The worship of any false god is, of course, hateful to the true God. We know that. To us, Baal worship seems like a disgusting and foolish practice. We are far too sophisticated to understand its appeal. But aren't false gods just as prevalent today as in Jezebel's day? Consider, for instance, the popularity of New Age religion or the way many worship sports heroes, movie stars, and millionaires. Ours, unfortunately, is a society that bows to gods of money, sex, and power. Anything, no matter how good, that supplants God's place in our lives can become an idol if we let it.

Jezebel's Legacy in Scripture

Read 1 Kings 16:31.

1. Many Israelite kings married foreign princesses to strengthen Israel's alliances with other countries, but Ahab's marriage to Jezebel gets special mention here. What does this tell you about Jezebel?

2. Jezebel's reputation in Scripture is one of sheer wickedness and selfishness. What reputation do you have with your family? With your church family? With your coworkers? With your friends? What can you do to make sure your reputation is one that honors God?

Read 1 Kings 18:4.

3. What does Jezebel's action in this verse tell you about her devotion to Baal?

4. What makes it obvious to people you meet that you serve the Lord?

Read 1 Kings 18:20–19:2.

5. Compare Jezebel's (19:2) and the Israelites' (18:39) reactions to the Mount Carmel duel. What do you think made Jezebel so dedicated to Baal?

6. How dedicated are you to the Lord? What might cause you to rethink that dedication?

Read 1 Kings 21:1–7.

7. What does this story tell you about Jezebel and Ahab? Who do you think was really ruling the nation? Compare 1 Kings 21:25.

Read 2 Kings 9:30–37.

8. What is significant about the fact that the Bible mentions that Jezebel "painted her eyes" and "arranged her hair"? What do you think Jezebel was getting ready for?

9. How do you get ready for a difficult situation? For conflict?

10. The story of Jezebel's demise is a disturbing one. She eventually got what we think she deserved, but consider: What do any of us truly deserve? And what, if we're followers of Christ, will we get instead?

28

THE WIDOW
OF ZAREPHATH

HER CHARACTER: A foreigner facing starvation, she showed extraordinary hospitality to one of God's prophets, providing a safe harbor for him.

KEY SCRIPTURES: 1 Kings 17:8–24; Luke 4:25–26

Then the word of the LORD came to [Elijah]: "Go at once to Zarephath of Sidon and stay there. I have commanded a widow in that place to supply you with food." So he went to Zarephath. When he came to the town gate, a widow was there gathering sticks. He called to her and asked, "Would you . . . bring me, please, a piece of bread."

"As surely as the LORD your God lives," she replied, "I don't have any bread—only a handful of flour in a jar and a little oil in a jug. I am gathering a few sticks to take home and make a meal for myself and my son, that we may eat it—and die."

Elijah said to her, "Don't be afraid. Go home and do as you have said. But first make a small cake of bread for me from what you have and bring it to me, and then make something for yourself and your son. For this is what the LORD, the God of Israel, says: 'The jar of flour will not be used up and the jug of oil will not run dry until the day the LORD gives rain on the land.'"

She went away and did as Elijah had told her. So there was food every day for Elijah and for the woman and her family.

1 KINGS 17:8–15

The Widow's Life and Times

Widows

The widow of Zarephath lived in a cruel and insensitive Phoenician society, one that treated widows as second-class citizens, ignored them, and allowed them to go hungry. When Elijah came and asked the widow for bread, it appeared as though he were asking her to give up the last food she had for herself and her son. Actually, he provided her with sustenance that would last until the famine was over.

Since a woman alone seldom had any way to provide financially for herself, she was dependent on her sons, if she had any, and on the community around her, if she didn't. The Bible tells how God himself has a special love and care for women who have lost their husbands (Psalm 68:5; 146:9). He commanded the Israelites to treat widows with compassion and to provide for them. When the prophets declared the Israelites to be disobedient, they often proved it by exposing their lack of concern for the widows around them (Isaiah 1:23; 10:1–2; Ezekiel 22:6–7; Malachi 3:5). When someone cared for the widowed, it was worthy of note (Job 29:13).

In the New Testament, Paul gave instructions to widows, telling them that if they were young, they should remarry. The church had to take care of a widow only if she was over sixty and had no other family members to take care of her (1 Timothy 5:3–16). The touching story of Dorcas in Acts 9:36–42 shows how much a simple act, done for a widow who is truly in need, can mean.

Our Life and Times

Today's church is also responsible for caring for the widows in their congregations. Often, insurance payments, Social Security, and the like may take care of a widow's financial needs, but her needs go far beyond having enough money in the checking account. Fellow believers can show their love by freely giving emotional support to the woman, by helping out physically with child care or household chores, or by providing friendship.

The Widow's Legacy in Scripture

Read 1 Kings 17.

1. Why is it surprising that God would send Elijah to a widow for food?

2. How has God provided for you in surprising ways?

3. The first words the widow speaks to the prophet Elijah (17:12) are words of searing honesty: Here is what I have left and here is what I'm planning to do. What is she telling Elijah with these words?

4. In today's generally abundant society, it is perhaps more difficult than ever to admit that you do not have enough and that you need help. When have you or someone you know had to be as honest as the widow about your needs? What did you learn from being put in this position?

5. Why do you think the widow went and did what Elijah asked her to do (17:13–14)? What did she have to lose?

6. Where was the widow placing blame for her son's death (17:18)? Her sin? Elijah's presence? God?

7. Now it is Elijah's turn to be completely honest (17:20). Why do you think Elijah was so desperate for the woman's son to return to life?

8. Have you ever been as desperate as Elijah? What circumstances in your life caused your desperation? What was God's answer?

9. Now, for a second time, the widow's son is saved by God through Elijah. What is the widow's response when her son is returned to her (17:24)?

10. Through this foreign woman God reveals his willingness to supply our needs if we will depend on him. Have you ever doubted God's ability or willingness to give you what you need?

29

THE SHUNAMMITE WOMAN

HER CHARACTER: Generous and hospitable, she was a wealthy and capable woman who showed great kindness to one of God's prophets.

KEY SCRIPTURES: 2 Kings 4:8–37; 2 Kings 8:1–6

One day Elisha went to Shunem. And a well-to-do woman was there, who urged him to stay for a meal. So whenever he came by, he stopped there to eat. She said to her husband, "I know that this man who often comes our way is a holy man of God. Let's make a small room on the roof and put in it a bed and a table, a chair and a lamp for him. Then he can stay there whenever he comes to us."

One day when Elisha came, he went up to his room and lay down there. He said to his servant Gehazi, "Call the Shunammite." So he called her, and she stood before him. Elisha said to him, "Tell her, 'You have gone to all this trouble for us. Now what can be done for you? Can we speak on your behalf to the king or the commander of the army?'"

She replied, "I have a home among my own people."

"What can be done for her?" Elisha asked.

Gehazi said, "Well, she has no son and her husband is old."

Then Elisha said, "Call her." So he called her, and she stood in the doorway. "About this time next year," Elisha said, "you will hold a son in your arms."

"No, my lord," she objected. "Don't mislead your servant, O man of God!"

But the woman became pregnant, and the next year about that same time she gave birth to a son, just as Elisha had told her.

―――― 2 KINGS 4:8–17 ――――

The Shunammite's Life and Times

Hospitality

Hospitality played an important role in the lives of the people of the Middle East. Desert travel was strenuous, and Holiday Inns hadn't yet been invented. When travelers came to a town at the end of the day, they would stop in the town's center or near the town gates and wait for an invitation for the night. If no invitation came, they would spend the night outside. Hosts were responsible not only to feed and provide sleeping arrangements for their guests but also were expected to ensure the safety of the guests, protecting them from robbery and harm (Genesis 19:8). When meals were served, the host watched guests closely to be sure their needs were being met. If one guest was particularly favored over another, he or she would be served an extra large or extra special portion of the food (Genesis 43:34).

Examples of hospitality are plentiful in the Scriptures. Abraham made a sumptuous meal for the three strangers who visited him (Genesis 18), preparing bread, a tender calf, curds, and milk. Rebekah practiced a basic form of hospitality when she offered a drink to Abraham's servant and his camels (Genesis 24:15–21). Solomon fed everyone in his palace, plus aliens and visitors to the region. His list of daily provisions in 1 Kings 4:22 provides a picture of feeding a staggering number of people. Nehemiah not only refused to demand "the food allotted to the governor," he also generously fed at least 150 each day (Nehemiah 5:17–18).

Our Life and Times

Six times the New Testament exhorts believers to be hospitable. There's no talk of fatted calves or extravagant dinners in these passages, just a simple exhortation to make sure those around you are taken care of. As Romans 12:13 puts it, "Share with God's people who are in need. Practice hospitality."

The Shunammite's Legacy in Scripture

Read 2 Kings 4:8–37.

1. Why do you think stopping at this woman's house became a habit for Elisha? Why do you think she wanted to go so far as to add on a room for him?

2. Have you ever been hospitable when it was difficult or inconvenient? Or are you hospitable only when it fits into your schedule? By this standard, how would you describe true hospitality?

3. Why do you think the Shunammite woman responded the way she did when Elisha told her she would have a child? What was she afraid of? See verse 28 also.

4. Why did the woman tell her husband and Gehazi that everything was "all right" when it obviously was not? What was her goal?

5. Have you ever been able to say, "It's all right" even when something bad has happened to you or to someone you love? Why would you say such a thing during a difficult time?

6. Why do you think the woman insisted Elisha go with her?

7. Who is an Elisha in your life—someone you immediately go to when you're in need of support and help?

30

ATHALIAH AND JEHOSHEBA

ATHALIAH

Her Name Means "The Lord Is Great"

HER CHARACTER: Granddaughter of Omri, one of Israel's most idolatrous and evil kings, she was the daughter of Ahab and most likely of Jezebel as well. She was the only woman to rule over Judah. While Ahab and Jezebel spread Baal worship in the northern kingdom of Israel, Athaliah was busy promoting it a few years later in the southern kingdom of Judah. Controlled by her need for power, she murdered her own family members to secure it.

KEY SCRIPTURES: 2 Kings 11; 2 Chronicles 22; 23:11–21

JEHOSHEBA

Her Name Means
"Swear by His Name"

HER CHARACTER: A princess and the wife of the high priest, she was a courageous woman whose actions preserved the line of Judah, from which the Messiah would come.

KEY SCRIPTURES: 2 Kings 11:2; 2 Chronicles 22:11

When Athaliah the mother of Ahaziah saw that her son was dead, she proceeded to destroy the whole royal family. But Jehosheba, the daughter of King Jehoram and sister of Ahaziah, took Joash son of Ahaziah and stole him away from among the royal princes, who were about to be murdered. She put him and his nurse in a bedroom to hide him from Athaliah; so he was not killed. He remained hidden with his nurse at the temple of the LORD for six years while Athaliah ruled the land.

In the seventh year Jehoiada sent for the commanders . . . and the guards and had them brought to him at the temple of the LORD. He made a covenant with them and put them under oath at the temple of the LORD. Then he showed them the king's son.

. . . Jehoiada brought out the king's son and put the crown on him; he presented him with a copy of the covenant and proclaimed him king. They anointed him, and the people clapped their hands and shouted, "Long live the king!"

When Athaliah heard the noise made by the guards and the people, she went to the people at the temple of the LORD. She looked and there was the king. . . . Then Athaliah tore her robes and called out, "Treason! Treason!"

Jehoiada the priest ordered the commanders. . . . So they seized her as she reached the place where the horses enter the palace grounds, and there she was put to death.

2 KINGS 11:1–4, 12–16

Notes

Athaliah's and Jehosheba's Life and Times

The Temple

Smart Jehosheba! She hid little Joash away in the place Baal-worshiping Athaliah was least likely to stumble on him: in the temple of the Lord. Though at times the people of Israel misused the temple to worship idols, it remained primarily a place for worship of the true God.

King David had been the one to begin making plans for a great temple to replace the tabernacle as a place for worship. The tabernacle was not a permanent building, and David thought it only fitting that God should have as magnificent a house as his own (2 Samuel 7:2). David gathered great stores of stone and iron and bronze and "more cedar logs than could be counted" (1 Chronicles 22:4) in preparation for building the temple. He also obtained "a hundred thousand talents of gold, a million talents of silver." Believe it or not, that's about 3,750 tons of gold and an astonishing 37,500 tons of silver!

David's son Solomon actually built the temple in Jerusalem. The building began during the fourth year of his reign (966 B.C.) and wasn't completed until the eleventh year. The structure was built of stone cut and dressed at quarries and transported to the temple site. The stone was then covered with cedar wood, carved with cherubim and palm trees and flowers, then covered with gold. A reading of 1 Kings 5:1–9:25 gives a marvelous picture of the lavish structure Solomon dedicated to the Lord.

Jehosheba and her husband the high priest hid the heir to the throne in that same structure. The temple now housed not only the presence of the true God, but also the ancestor of God's Son, Jesus the Messiah. Through the brave actions of one woman, the lineage of David was protected and our salvation through the Messiah was assured.

Athaliah's and Jehosheba's Legacy in Scripture

Read 2 Kings 11:1–3.

1. Who might be included here? Other sons? Grandsons? What would cause such a total loss of natural affection that Athaliah could do such a thing?

2. Have you ever been so eager to get your own way that you did something you're not proud of, even ashamed to admit you did? What was it? What was the outcome?

3. Why do you think Jehosheba saved only Joash (11:2)? What might have been going through her mind during these events?

4. Recall a time in your life when you bravely did what was right. Was it hard or easy? What was the result?

5. For six years God allowed Athaliah to reign unopposed while young prince Joash hid (11:3). Have you ever had to wait for God's plan to be fulfilled? Six years? Longer? Describe what you learned.

Read 2 Kings 11:4–20.

6. Verses 4–12 contain details of the careful preparations Jehoiada made before showing young Joash to anyone. Why would such preparations be necessary? What would have happened if Joash had been killed?

7. Note Athaliah's response when she sees the child-king (11:14). How could she have responded differently? Why did she respond as she did?

8. Every situation can bring different responses from us. Describe a difficult situation in your life and list possible responses to that situation. Which response did you choose? Was it the right one? Why or why not?

9. Why was this a victory for the Lord as well as for the monarchy?

10. In verse 17 the people make a covenant, a promise, to be "the Lord's people." If you have ever made such a promise, what has it meant in your life?

31

HULDAH

Her Name Means "Weasel"

HER CHARACTER: Trusted by the king with a matter of great importance, she was a prophetess whose word generated a significant religious reform.

KEY SCRIPTURES: 2 Kings 22:14–20; 2 Chronicles 34:22–33

Notes

⌇

When [Josiah] heard the words of the Law, he tore his robes. He gave these orders . . . "Go and inquire of the LORD . . . about what is written in this book that has been found. Great is the LORD's anger that is poured out on us because our fathers have not kept the word of the LORD." . . .

Those the king had sent . . . went to speak to the prophetess Huldah. . . .

She said to them, "This is what the LORD, the God of Israel, says: Tell the man who sent you to me, 'This is what the LORD says: I am going to bring disaster on this place and its people . . . because they have forsaken me and burned incense to other gods. . . . Tell the king of Judah . . . because your heart was responsive and you humbled yourself before God . . . I will gather you to your fathers, and you will be buried in peace.'"

——— 2 CHRONICLES 34:19–28 ———

Huldah's Life and Times

Books and Scrolls

Ancient writers recorded their thoughts and information on clay tablets. Literally hundreds of thousands of these tablets have been found, many of which have yet to be read. And it is estimated that ninety-nine percent of the ancient tablets still in existence have yet to be found.

Later, writers wrote on scrolls. The paper for the scrolls was made from sheets of the papyrus reed, which grew along the Nile River. The separate pieces were glued together into one long sheet and then rolled onto wooden dowels, with the beginning of the scroll on the right and the end on the left. Readers, usually men and sometimes boys—girls were seldom taught to read—read the columns of letters from top to bottom, right to left. The reader would roll up the read portion of the scroll while unrolling the unread portion.

After some time the Israelites formed another sort of paper, called parchment, from the skins of animals. They were careful to use only skins from clean animals for the paper to be used to record the Scriptures. The animal skins were treated until they were supple and very light in color, and then several of these prepared skins would be sewn together to form one scroll. For instance, an old copy of the book of Isaiah found as part of the Dead Sea Scrolls in 1947 is a scroll made of seventeen pieces of skin of varying sizes sewn together. The scroll is about ten inches wide and an amazing twenty-four feet long when unrolled.

Books as we know them today, with page after page bound together between two covers, did not develop until the second century A.D. Original copies, called autographs, of the Old and New Testaments no longer exist. Parchment and papyrus both decay when exposed to age and dampness. Also, New Testament books and letters may literally have been read to pieces or may have been destroyed during times of persecution.

The Book of the Law discovered in the temple during Josiah's day was probably made from papyrus. Historians are uncertain exactly how much of the law was contained in this scroll. Some think it contained the entire Pentateuch (Genesis through Deuteronomy), while others believe it only contained the book of Deuteronomy. Josiah's reaction, however, would cause one to believe that at least the curses of Leviticus 26 or Deuteronomy 28 were included.

Huldah, the faithful prophetess during a time of national unfaithfulness, bravely spoke God's judgment. She emphasized the words of judgment Josiah had already read in the Book of the Law, and then went on to pronounce a reprieve for Josiah because of his sorrow over the sins of his people. Once again, God had faithfully and wonderfully demonstrated his divine judgment as well as his divine willingness to forgive.

Huldah's Legacy in Scripture

Read 2 Kings 22:11–20.

1. Judah had followed false gods for many years. What do you think made Josiah receptive to God and this reading of his law?

2. Think of a time when you were tremendously sorry for your past or for something you had done. How did you pray? How did you feel?

3. Describe what you think Huldah might have been like: her person, her character, her relationship with God (22:14).

4. What about your description of Huldah would you like to be true of you? What can you do to develop that part of your character?

5. Why was God so angry with his people (22:17)? What was he planning to do?

6. What has our nation done that deserves God's judgment?

7. What was God's specific word to Josiah (22:19)? Why was God's response to Josiah different from his response to the people?

8. What have you done that deserves God's judgment? Do you think God's response to you will be like his response to Josiah or to the people? What will make the difference?

32

GOMER

Her Name Means "Completion"

HER CHARACTER: Though a married woman, she carried on numerous love affairs, crediting her lovers for the gifts her husband had given her.

KEY SCRIPTURE: Hosea 1–3

➤

When the LORD began to speak through Hosea, the LORD said to him, "Go, take to yourself an adulterous wife and children of unfaithfulness, because the land is guilty of the vilest adultery in departing from the LORD." So he married Gomer.

. . . The LORD said to me, "Go, show your love to your wife again, though she is loved by another and is an adulteress. Love her as the LORD loves the Israelites, though they turn to other gods and love the sacred raisin cakes."

So I bought her for fifteen shekels of silver and about a homer and a lethek of barley. Then I told her, "You are to live with me many days; you must not be a prostitute or be intimate with any man, and I will live with you."

For the Israelites will live many days without king or prince, without sacrifice or sacred stones, without ephod or idol. Afterward the Israelites will return and seek the LORD their God and David their king. They will come trembling to the LORD and to his blessings in the last days.

─── HOSEA 1:2–3; 3:1–5 ───

Gomer's Life and Times

Prophets

Gomer's husband Hosea appeared on the scene as the last of the prophets who spoke the "word of the Lord" (Hosea 1:1) to the doomed northern kingdom. Before long, the Assyrians would conquer the capital of Samaria and take thousands of Israelites captive. When the book of Hosea begins with "the word of the Lord," it asserts Hosea's authority as a prophet, that God has spoken to him and that he must relay the message to the people.

The Israelites in Palestine had the law God had given to Moses and the people at Sinai. This consisted of the Ten Commandments as well as the other rules for living included in the books of Moses (Genesis through Deuteronomy). However, those laws didn't cover many of life's situations and decisions. God instituted the office of the prophet for the many times when a specific revelation of God was needed for the people to know what they should do next.

We don't always know how prophets received their messages from God. At times, visions and dreams gave the message. Ezekiel and Daniel both record visions that contained a definite message from God. Other times, as in Hosea, the prophets simply declared that their words were from the Lord. The emphasis of God's prophets was never on the method of receiving his word—whether mysterious or obvious—but on the message itself and on the people's need to follow. God made it very clear that if the people would only listen and obediently follow the words of the prophets, he would give them all they needed to face an unknown future.

Our Life and Times

Just as God provided for his people in the Promised Land, he has provided for us. He may not miraculously reveal the path or supernaturally tell us his will, as he did with the Israelites, but he has revealed himself and his plans for us through the Bible, and his messengers today underscore and explain what Scripture tells us. We can be assured that God will go with us, just as he went with the Israelites, holding our hands as we face whatever our futures hold.

Gomer's Legacy in Scripture

Read Hosea 1:1–9.

1. Compare verse 1 with Deuteronomy 18:21–22. How could the people know Hosea actually spoke "the word of the Lord"?

2. When a minister or evangelist speaks the word of the Lord today, how can you know if it's true or not? What can you measure his or her words against to be sure they are from the Lord?

3. What sin is the Lord accusing his people of committing (1:2)?

4. How would you compare the people of Israel and their sins with the nation you live in today? How is your nation like Israel? How is it different? What do you think God would say through Hosea to your nation?

5. What do each of the names of Hosea's children signify (1:4, 6, 9)? How clear should that message have been to the people of Israel?

6. How does God speak to us today? How clear is his message? Are we any better at understanding and following than the Israelites were?

Read Hosea 1:10–2:1.

7. Put these beautiful words of God for his people into your own words.

8. What do these words mean for you today? How has God been faithful to you even when you were unfaithful to him?

Read Hosea 3:1–5.

9. In this chapter, Hosea's relationship with his adulterous wife is again compared to God's relationship with the unfaithful Israelites. Did Gomer return of her own accord or did Hosea go out and seek her?

10. Note especially the word *bought* (3:2). Hosea paid fifteen shekels (about six ounces) of silver, plus about ten bushels of barley for Gomer. Just as Hosea will go to extreme lengths to get his wife back—not so much *what* he paid for her, but the very fact that he paid—God will go to extreme lengths to get his people back. What ultimate price did God pay for his people?

33

ESTHER

Her Name May Derive from "Ishtar,"
the Babylonian ... Goddess of ... Love, or from the Persian Word for "Star."
Her Hebrew Name, "Hadassah," Means "Myrtle"

HER CHARACTER: An orphan in a foreign land, she displayed great courage in the midst of a crisis. Prior to risking her life for her people, she humbled herself by fasting, and then put her considerable beauty, social grace, and wisdom in the service of God's plan.

KEY SCRIPTURE: Esther 1–10

>

Mordecai had a cousin named [Esther], whom he had brought up because she had neither father nor mother. This girl . . . was lovely in form and features. . . .

Esther . . . was taken to the king's palace and entrusted to Hegai, who had charge of the harem. The girl pleased him and won his favor. Immediately he provided her with her beauty treatments and special food. He assigned to her seven maids selected from the king's palace and moved her and her maids into the best place in the harem.

Now the king was attracted to Esther more than to any of the other women. . . . So he set a royal crown on her head and made her queen. . . .

Mordecai told [Hathach] everything that had happened to him, including the exact amount of money Haman had promised to pay into the royal treasury for the destruction of the Jews. He . . . told [Hathach] to urge [Esther] to go into the king's presence to beg for mercy and plead with him for her people.

Then Esther sent this reply to Mordecai: "Go, gather together all the Jews who are in Susa, and fast for me. Do not eat or drink for three days, night or day. I and my maids will fast as you do. When this is done, I will go to the king, even though it is against the law. And if I perish, I perish."

—— ESTHER 2:7–9, 17; 4:7–8, 15–16 ——

Esther's Life and Times

The Festival of Purim

When Haman threw the lot or the *pur* to discover what day would be the best day to annihilate the Jews in Xerxes' kingdom, he unwittingly established a festival called Purim, when, instead of annihilation, the Jews celebrated their deliverance. Esther and her cousin Mordecai jointly worked to overturn Haman's plot, and when they were successful, sent out a proclamation to all the Jews living in Xerxes' kingdom to "celebrate annually the fourteenth and fifteenth days of the month of Adar as the time when the Jews got relief from their enemies, and as the month when their sorrow was turned into joy and their mourning into a day of celebration" (Esther 9:21–22).

Adar 14 and 15. Adar was the last month in the Jewish calendar—our February/March. Josephus, the first-century Jewish general and historian, claimed that Jews all over the world celebrated the Festival of Purim in his day, and it continues to be a popular festival for Jews today. (For a chart on the Jewish calendar, turn to page 233.)

Worship and fasting typically make up the first day of the festival. The entire book of Esther is read aloud, and the congregation responds with "Let his name be blotted out" each time Haman's name is read. The children in the group respond to Haman's name with noisemakers and rattles. On the second day of the feast, rejoicing and celebration break out. Food, music, dramas and plays, special songs, and recitals all add to the festive mood. People give gifts to each other and also make sure they don't forget to give gifts and food to the poor, as that was a special wish of Mordecai (Esther 9:22).

Like the Passover, the Feast of Purim celebrates divine deliverance. Saved from Pharaoh's rule and slavery in Egypt and delivered from the destruction planned by Haman, the Jews celebrated a deliverance that only God could have orchestrated. Previously doomed, they were now delivered.

Esther's Legacy in Scripture

Read the entire book of Esther, in one sitting if possible.

1. Examine each of the main characters of the story and list one or two primary characteristics of each character:

   Vashti

   Xerxes

   Esther

   Mordecai

   Haman

2. With which character do you identify most closely?

3. Esther's royal position was no accident. She was in a position of influence for a very specific purpose. Your position in life is not an accident either. What do you think God might have for you to do right where you are, right now?

4. Have you ever had to be brave like Esther to step out and do the right thing? What were the circumstances? What was the outcome?

5. How have you been delivered like the Jews in this story? How do you celebrate your deliverance?

34

THE WOMAN
OF PROVERBS 31

Notes

HER CHARACTER: She represents the fulfillment of a life lived in wisdom.

KEY SCRIPTURE: Proverbs 31:10–31

A wife of noble character who can find?
  She is worth far more than rubies.
Her husband has full confidence in her
  and lacks nothing of value.
She brings him good, not harm,
  all the days of her life. . . .
She is clothed with strength and dignity;
  she can laugh at the days to come.
She speaks with wisdom,
  and faithful instruction is on her tongue. . . .
Her children arise and call her blessed;
  her husband also, and he praises her:
"Many women do noble things,
  but you surpass them all."

PROVERBS 31:10–12, 25–26, 28–29

The Proverbs 31 Woman's Life and Times

Spinning and Weaving

The woman of Proverbs 31 was a real pro at working with fabrics. She started by selecting the wool and flax (verse 13), then spun it into threads (verse 19). She wove the woolen threads into rich scarlet clothing to keep her family warm in snowy weather (verse 21). She wove the flax threads into linen for bed coverings, fine clothing for herself, and clothing and sashes to sell (verse 22).

Traditionally women's work, the spinning and weaving of cloth for clothing, bedding, rugs, and other needs occupied a tremendous amount of the time and talents of Hebrew women. Fibers from plants like cotton and flax or wool from sheep were spun and twisted to produce a long thread. That thread could then be used to sew fabrics together with needles made of bone or it could be used to weave new fabric. Weaving, an art that the Hebrews probably perfected while they were in Egypt, was done on a rudimentary loom.

Old Testament families used fabrics for a variety of purposes. The oldest and most common fabric in biblical times was wool. Woolen fabrics were woven from the hair of lambs and sheep and were made into the everyday clothing worn by the common person, even in hot weather. Linen, which was woven from the flax plant, formed the fabrics from which inner clothing was made. Some linen was so finely woven that it formed a silky, translucent cloth from which the rich made their garments. Heavy cloth woven from goat or camel hair formed waterproof tents and outer clothing.

Sound like a lot of work? It was. The women of a household spent virtually every spare moment on one part or another of the task of making fabrics. The "wife of noble character" in Proverbs 31 works "with eager hands" (verse 13), and it seems as if the spindle and distaff never leave her fingers (verse 19). That's why "she has no fear for her household" (verse 21). Spinning and weaving have kept her busy all the time, but she and her family are ready for the cold weather.

Our Life and Times

Does just reading about the Proverbs 31 woman make you tired? Do you wish she would just sit down and rest a moment? Whatever your response to this larger-than-life woman, you can't help but notice that she never wasted the time given her. In our convenient culture of store-bought clothing and fast-food restaurants, you may not need to weave your own cloth or cook your own meals—but that's not the issue. The issue is whether we're making good use of the time given to us.

The Proverbs 31 Woman's Legacy in Scripture

Read Proverbs 31:10–31.

1. Describe the relationship between this woman and her husband (31:11–12).

2. What aspects of their relationship do you wish were part of your relationship with your husband, if you are married? What can you do to improve your relationship in that area?

3. List some of the different tasks that keep this woman busy (31:13–22, 24, 27). Now list *how* she goes about her work.

4. What keeps you busy? In what ways can you improve your attitude about your work?

5. Why can the woman of Proverbs 31 "laugh at the days to come" (31:25)? Doesn't she have anything to worry about? Why or why not?

6. What worries you? What can you do to be more like the woman of Proverbs 31 and "laugh at the days to come"?

7. What do this woman's children and husband do when she comes into the room (31:28)? Why do you think they are so respectful? What do you think the woman of Proverbs 31 has done to earn such praise from her husband and children?

8. Does verse 28 seem out of touch with reality to you? Why? What would you have to do or how would you have to change for this verse to be more of a reality in your life?

9. What is the thing that is most praiseworthy in any woman (31:30)? What if she isn't much of a housekeeper or isn't handy at crafts or isn't very good looking? What would make her still worthy of praise?

10. What's most important to you? Charm? Beauty? The fear of the Lord? How is that evident in your day-to-day life?

35

THE SHULAMMITE WOMAN

HER CHARACTER: Hers is the only female voice that speaks directly to us in the Scripture. Ruth's and Esther's voices, for instance, are mediated by narrators. The Shulammite woman boldly declares her longing and desire to be united to her lover in marriage.

KEY SCRIPTURE: Song of Songs 1–8

Place me like a seal over your heart,
*   like a seal on your arm;*
for love is as strong as death,
*   its jealousy unyielding as the grave.*
It burns like blazing fire,
*   like a mighty flame.*
Many waters cannot quench love;
*   rivers cannot wash it away.*
If one were to give
*   all the wealth of his house for love,*
*   it would be utterly scorned.*

SONG OF SONGS 8:6–7

The Shulammite Woman's Life and Times

Romantic Love

The erotic poetry of Song of Songs is not merely an expression of sexual desire but of the romantic love between a young man and a young woman. The love between the lover and the beloved is not merely one of physical pleasure and intimacy but one of a depth of feeling and commitment. True love doesn't fade with the changes brought about by time but is stronger even than death. Neither the waters of time nor the rivers of disappointment or tragedy can wash it away.

Most marriages in biblical times were arranged. When children were very young, their parents formed alliances to provide wives and husbands for their children. Many of these marriages took place when the participants were very young, so young that the rabbis eventually established the minimum age for marriage at twelve for girls and thirteen for boys. Although they were mere children even then, romantic and committed love developed over the years of marriage.

Although not all marriages were love matches from the beginning, many arranged marriages were eventually characterized by love. Isaac loved the wife his father's servant had gotten for him (Genesis 24:67). Elkanah loved Hannah, a wife he probably received by arrangement with her family (1 Samuel 1:5). A beautiful example of the sacrificial love of a husband for his wife is given in Exodus 21:2–5, where a husband willingly goes into servitude for life rather than leaving the wife he loves.

A man could, however, choose his own bride, even against the desires or arrangements of his parents. Jacob wanted to marry Rachel because he loved her (Genesis 29:18) and got her sister Leah also as part of the bargain. Samson begged his father to get a young Philistine woman for him, certain she was the right one for him (Judges 14:3).

The Old Testament seems to assume that husbands will love their wives, whether chosen by or for them. The Teacher in Ecclesiastes tells husbands to be sure to "enjoy life with your wife, whom you love" (Ecclesiastes 9:9), as though a husband's love for his wife is a given. The New Testament, however, urges husbands to love their wives. Four separate and clear times (Ephesians 5:25, 28, 33; Colossians 3:19) Paul mentions that husbands should love their wives, once even comparing that love to the love Christ has for his church.

Our Life and Times

If you have been so blessed in your own marriage to experience a love even half as passionate as the one described in this book of the Bible, read

Notes

it in light of your story, thanking God for his blessing. But even if you haven't, you can be glad that married love and its sexual expression was God's idea to begin with. You can also read the Song of Songs as a dialogue between God and your own soul. God's love, after all, is more passionate than any human love you could ever experience. He is the true Lover of your soul, ready to sing with you the greatest and most beautiful song of all.

The Shulammite Woman's Legacy in Scripture

Read the entire book of Song of Songs. (If you are married, read it with your husband, if he is willing.)

1. Song of Songs is, of course, very different from the love poems we know today; however, it is very descriptive and amorous. Choose one or two passages you think accurately describe the love relationship, physical and intimate, between a husband and a wife. If you can, put those ancient words into your own words.

2. Many of the images used in this poem give, indirectly, the idea of lengths of time spent together: "resting" (1:13); "sit" (2:3); "browse" (2:16; 6:2); "go"; "spend the night"; and "go early" (7:11–12). The impression is of long lengths of time spent together quietly and intimately. What picture does that give you of the love between this man and woman? What does it tell you about the need for time together with the one you love?

3. Song of Songs 8:6–7 expresses the undying commitment of the lover and the beloved. What do you think is required to have the love described in these verses? Is it something that just happens or is it something that must be worked out? Give reasons for your answers.

4. Throughout history, intimate love relationships have been shamefully distorted and profaned. Song of Songs gives God's picture of the beauty of the relationship. What can you do to foster this purer love in your own marriage relationship?

36

ELIZABETH

Her Name Means
"God Is My Oath"

Notes

HER CHARACTER: A descendant of Aaron, Elizabeth was a woman the Bible calls "upright in the sight of God." Like very few others, male or female, she is praised for observing all the Lord's commandments and regulations without blame. She is the first to acknowledge Jesus as Lord.

KEY SCRIPTURE: Luke 1:5–80

Elizabeth became pregnant and for five months remained in seclusion. "The Lord has done this for me," she said. "In these days he has shown his favor and taken away my disgrace among the people."

. . . Mary got ready and hurried to a town in the hill country of Judea, where she entered Zechariah's home and greeted Elizabeth. When Elizabeth heard Mary's greeting, the baby leaped in her womb, and Elizabeth was filled with the Holy Spirit. In a loud voice she exclaimed: "Blessed are you among women, and blessed is the child you will bear! But why am I so favored, that the mother of my Lord should come to me? As soon as the sound of your greeting reached my ears, the baby in my womb leaped for joy. Blessed is she who has believed that what the Lord has said to her will be accomplished!"

LUKE 1:24–25, 39–45

Elizabeth's Life and Times

I n c e n s e

Elizabeth's husband, Zechariah, had been given a very special, very serious privilege. When it was his priestly division's turn to serve in the temple, he was chosen by lot—which was God's way of making the choice—to burn incense in the temple. Each morning and evening he took fire from the altar of burnt offering and placed it on the golden altar of incense that stood before the curtain separating the Holy Place from the Most Holy Place. He then poured the dusty incense from a golden urn onto the fire. While Zechariah performed this duty, all the worshipers who were at the temple that day stood outside and prayed. The smoke and aroma of the incense symbolized their prayers rising up to God. The fragrance also served to fumigate air tainted with the odor of the blood of animals killed for the sacrifices.

The earliest historical records about worship include information on the burning of incense. All the nations surrounding Palestine appreciated the sweet smell of incense permeating not only their places of worship but also their homes. The incense Zechariah burned in the temple was made according to a special "recipe" (Exodus 30:34–38) of spices and salt that had been ground to a powder. This holy incense could be used only in the temple in worship, never for ordinary, everyday purposes.

The prophet Jeremiah often condemned the Israelites for burning incense to false gods. But he could be even more scathing in his denunciation when they burned incense when their hearts weren't in their worship (Jeremiah 6:20). God made it clear that the mere burning of incense didn't please him; it was only a symbol. He was looking for hearts that were turned toward him in faithfulness and trust.

Elizabeth's Legacy in Scripture

Read Luke 1:5–25.

1. What important things do these verses tell you about Elizabeth and Zechariah? Do you think the words of verse 6 mean they were perfect? If not, what *do* these words mean?

2. Why do you think Zechariah didn't believe the angel (1:18)? Was he so afraid? Was the announcement so unbelievable? Why do you think he was punished for not believing?

3. Imagine an angel coming to you with some unexpected and unbelievable announcement. What would your reaction be?

4. Why would Elizabeth say she was disgraced among her people (1:25)?

5. Describe how the infertile woman feels today. Is disgrace a part of her feelings? If you know someone who is struggling with infertility, how can you be a friend and support to her?

Read Luke 1:39–45.

6. Do you think the reaction of Elizabeth's baby to Mary's arrival was just coincidence? What do you think prompted the baby to "leap" just then (1:41)?

7. Elizabeth didn't just smile and offer a quiet prayer when Mary arrived. She "exclaimed" and praised God "in a loud voice" (1:42). What would have to happen for you to exclaim your praise to God in a loud voice?

8. What is the focus of Elizabeth's praise in verse 45: what God has done in *her* life or what God has done in *Mary's* life? What does this reveal about Elizabeth?

37

MARY, THE MOTHER OF JESUS

Her Name May Mean "Bitterness"

HER CHARACTER: She was a virgin from a poor family in an obscure village in Galilee. Her response to Gabriel reveals a young woman of unusual faith and humility. Her unqualified yes to God's plan for her life entailed great personal risk and suffering. She must have endured seasons of confusion, fear, and darkness as the events of her life unfolded. She is honored, not only as the mother of Jesus, but as his first disciple.

KEY SCRIPTURES: Matthew 1:18–25; 2; Luke 1:26–80; 2; John 19:25–27

This is how the birth of Jesus Christ came about: His mother Mary was pledged to be married to Joseph, but before they came together, she was found to be with child through the Holy Spirit. Because Joseph her husband was a righteous man and did not want to expose her to public disgrace, he had in mind to divorce her quietly.

But . . . an angel of the Lord appeared to him in a dream and said, "Joseph son of David, do not be afraid to take Mary home as your wife, because what is conceived in her is from the Holy Spirit. She will give birth to a son, and you are to give him the name Jesus, because he will save his people from their sins." . . .

When Joseph woke up, he did what the angel of the Lord had commanded him and took Mary home as his wife.

MATTHEW 1:18–21, 24

Mary's Life and Times

Angels

Mary cowered in fear when the angel Gabriel appeared to her—not an uncommon reaction. Most often in Scripture, when an angel appeared to a human being, the reaction was one of fright. While we're not told exactly what angels look like or how they appear, one description in Matthew says the angel's "appearance was like lightning, and his clothes were white as snow" (Matthew 28:3). Certainly it's obvious from the reactions of those who saw them that angels are supernatural beings and therefore frightening.

The 291 references to angels in Scripture give us a varied picture of the duties of angels. Angels in heaven stand before God's throne and worship him (Matthew 18:10). An angel helped Hagar and Ishmael when they were in trouble in the desert (Genesis 21:17). An angel freed the apostles from prison (Acts 5:19). An angel directed Philip to the desert road where he met and witnessed to the Ethiopian eunuch (Acts 8:26). An angel appeared to Paul to comfort him (Acts 27:23–24) and to Elijah when he was worn out and discouraged in the desert (1 Kings 19:3–9). Sometimes angels interpret God's message, as in Daniel's dreams, and sometimes God uses angels to punish his enemies (Genesis 19:1; 2 Kings 19:35).

Angels played an important role in the life of Jesus. After first appearing to Zechariah, Mary, and Joseph, angels announced Jesus' birth to the shepherds (Luke 2:9). Angels came and ministered to Jesus after he was tempted in the desert (Matthew 4:11) and when he was in the garden just before his crucifixion (Luke 22:43). A violent earthquake accompanied the angel that came to earth and rolled back the stone over Jesus' tomb (Matthew 28:2). When Jesus ascended into heaven, two angels, "men dressed in white" (Acts 1:10), told the disciples he would be coming back in the same way.

In the book of Revelation, John describes a glorious scene: "Then I looked and heard the voice of many angels, numbering thousands upon thousands, and ten thousand times ten thousand. They encircled the throne and the living creatures and the elders. In a loud voice they sang: 'Worthy is the Lamb, who was slain, to receive power and wealth and wisdom and strength and honor and glory and praise!'" (Revelation 5:11–12).

Our Life and Times

Imagine the sight: hundreds of thousands of beings—purest white, like lightning—all moving in concert around God's throne. Listen: can you imagine their loud, supernatural voices praising Jesus? *Worthy is the Lamb!* Then "every creature in heaven and on earth and under the earth and on the sea, and all that is in them" (Revelation 5:13) will join in with them, singing the same song of praise. What a sight! What a sound! Mary will be there praising her son. Will you be there praising your Savior?

Mary's Legacy in Scripture

Read Luke 1:26–38.

1. Put the angel's greetings into your own words (1:28). Why do you think this greeting troubled Mary?

2. If an angel were to visit you today, what sort of greeting do you think he would give you? What would the greeting reveal about your character and about your relationship with God?

3. What two things does the angel tell Mary in verses 36 and 37? Why would he tell her about Elizabeth? Why would he tell her that "nothing is impossible with God"? Didn't Mary already know this?

4. If truly "nothing is impossible with God," what area of your life or circumstance do you need to turn over to him? What is keeping you from doing this?

5. What does Mary's response tell you about her (1:38)? Do you think at this point she truly realizes what her future holds? How will the attitude apparent in these words help her in the difficult times in the future?

Read Luke 2:1–7.

6. These words are so familiar and the story so well-known. The birth of God on earth becomes commonplace, ordinary. Reread these verses, considering while you do the emotions Joseph and Mary must have experienced, what they might have said to each other, how they might have prayed. Then contemplate the actual event: not just the birth of a baby but the birth of the Christ!

Read Luke 2:41–52.

7. Who does Mary call Jesus' father? Who does Jesus say his father is? Why is this significant?

8. Verse 50 says Mary and Joseph "did not understand" what Jesus meant by what he said to them. However, verse 51 says that Mary "treasured all these things in her heart." Contrast the two verses. What do you think is meant by "treasured"?

Read John 19:25–27.

9. It is pretty hard to put into words the agony Mary must have been experiencing as she watched her son die. Seeing her distress must have added to Jesus' torment. What does this scene tell you about their relationship?

10. Watching a son or daughter die is perhaps the most painful experience known to the human race. Where is the only place one can go to find some comfort when such painful events enter our lives? Why?

38

ANNA

Her Name Means
"Favor" or "Grace"

HER CHARACTER: Married for only seven years, she spent the long years of her widowhood fasting and praying in the temple, abandoning herself entirely to God. A prophetess, she was one of the first to bear witness to Jesus.

KEY SCRIPTURE: Luke 2:22–38

When the time of their purification according to the Law of Moses had been completed, Joseph and Mary took [Jesus] to Jerusalem to present him to the Lord.

[In Jerusalem] there was . . . a prophetess, Anna. . . . She was very old; she had lived with her husband seven years after her marriage, and then was a widow until she was eighty-four. She never left the temple but worshiped night and day, fasting and praying. Coming up to them at that very moment, she gave thanks to God and spoke about the child to all who were looking forward to the redemption of Jerusalem.

LUKE 2:22, 36–38

Anna's Life and Times

The Temple Courts

The old woman Anna had probably spent upwards of sixty years in the temple. In fact, she never left it, "but worshiped night and day, fasting and praying" (Luke 2:37). The evidence of her devotion is not just in the fact that she spent all those years in prayer, but that she *recognized* the Christ. (He was, after all, only about six weeks old.) Yet even though Anna had relinquished a normal lifestyle, spent hours of every day in prayer to her God, and went without food as a sign of devotion, she was still not allowed access to the actual temple. Despite being relegated to the outer court for women, however, she never let that restriction squeeze her heart or strangle her love for God.

Solomon had built the first temple, an elaborate, white limestone structure, inlaid with gold. Zerubbabel built the second temple when the Jews returned from captivity in Babylon. This structure was not nearly so imposing. In fact, those who had seen Solomon's temple wept when they saw the foundation for the new temple (Ezra 3:12–13). Herod the Great built the temple where Anna worshiped. He was a tireless builder, and the temple in Jerusalem was only one of his projects.

Herod's temple had four successive courts, each more exclusive than the one before it. The outer court was known as the Court of the Gentiles. This was the only place where non-Jews were allowed. This court was also the place where Jesus later cleared the temple of those buying and selling. The inner court was divided into two sections: the Women's Court, where Anna worshiped, and the Court of Israel. Both Jewish women and men could enter the Women's Court, but only Jewish men were allowed into the Court of Israel. The Court of the Priests surrounded the actual temple building itself and was accessible only to those of the Levitical priesthood.

Our Life and Times

The customs of her time may have restricted the physical location of Anna's worship, but no earthly regulation could bind her actual worship or devotion. Be an Anna! Don't let anything bind your devotion to God! No earthly rules or restrictions. No past mistakes or sins. No life situations that you can't overcome. Let nothing get in the way of worshiping your God and recognizing your Savior.

Anna's Legacy in Scripture

Read Luke 2:22–38.

1. What does their careful observance of the Law of Moses tell you about Joseph and Mary?

2. What about your life reveals your Christian commitment?

3. What did Simeon's words reveal about himself (2:29–32)? What did they reveal about Jesus' life and ministry?

4. The promise Simeon held onto was that he would see the Christ before he died (2:26). If you knew death were near, what would you like to see God accomplish before you died?

5. What do you think Simeon meant when he told Mary that "a sword will pierce your . . . soul" (2:35)?

6. Describe what you think Anna's lifestyle was like.

7. What about Anna's lifestyle do you wish were true of your own? What can you do to make that happen in your life?

8. What do you think Anna said about Jesus? How do you think the crowd who listened responded?

9. If an Anna were to have spoken (prophesied) about you when you were six weeks old, what might she have said?

39

THE WOMAN
OF SAMARIA

HER CHARACTER: Looked down on by the Jews because she was a Samaritan, and disdained because of her many romantic liaisons, she would not have been most people's first choice to advance the gospel in a region where it had not yet been heard.

KEY SCRIPTURE: John 4:1–42

When a Samaritan woman came to draw water, Jesus said to her, "Will you give me a drink?"

. . . The Samaritan woman said to him, "You are a Jew and I am a Samaritan woman. How can you ask me for a drink?" (For Jews do not associate with Samaritans.)

Jesus answered her, "If you knew the gift of God and who it is that asks you for a drink, you would have asked him and he would have given you living water."

. . . The woman said to him, "Sir, give me this water so that I won't get thirsty and have to keep coming here to draw water."

. . . Jesus declared, "Believe me . . . a time is coming and has now come when the true worshipers will worship the Father in spirit and truth, for they are the kind of worshipers the Father seeks. God is spirit, and his worshipers must worship in spirit and in truth."

The woman said, "I know that Messiah" (called Christ) "is coming. When he comes, he will explain everything to us."

Then Jesus declared, "I who speak to you am he."

JOHN 4:7, 9–10, 15, 21, 23–26

The Woman of Samaria's Life and Times

Water

Cool, clear water. A commodity most of us today take for granted. We turn on a faucet, and water is readily available. In Palestine, however, water is scarce and valued.

The long, mostly rainless summers cause most of the rivers in Palestine to dry up completely. Even the Jordan River becomes shallow, narrow, and muddy in the summer months. The early peoples of Palestine depended on rain during the spring and fall months for their water supply. Though scarce at other times during the year, the rain during these seasons kept the springs and wells flowing and cisterns full.

The Jews became adept at gathering every bit of rainwater, storing it up for future use during the dry seasons. Cisterns, covered pools dug out of rock specifically for storing rainwater, were numerous. In Jerusalem, the temple area alone had thirty-seven cisterns, one of them large enough to hold over two million gallons of water. Gutters, pipes, and waterways directed the rainwater from the surface to the underground cistern, which would provide a constant supply of water, even during dry spells.

Heavy dew provided a good share of the moisture required by crops growing in the summer months. The warm, cloudless nights of Palestinian summers provide prime conditions for dew to form. Where ample water was readily available, farmers irrigated crops and vineyards to maximize the produce received from a field.

Drinking water was stored and carried in goatskins. Many towns and cities had drinking water for sale in their markets and on the streets. Only a minimal amount of water was used for washing, simply because it was so scarce. However, good hospitality required that a guest in someone's home receive a basin of water to wash at least his or her feet and hands after walking on the dusty roads (Genesis 18:4; John 13:5).

Getting daily water from the neighborhood well or cistern was the duty of the younger women of a household. They would usually go to the well in the evening, when the air was cooler. It's interesting to note that the Samaritan woman went to the well at noon ("the sixth hour"), probably in order to avoid the other women, who may have looked down on her.

Water is used in symbolic ways throughout Scripture. David compared his troubles to "deep waters" (Psalm 69:1–2, 14; 124:5). The book of Proverbs compares people's words to deep waters and wise words to "bubbling brooks" of water (Proverbs 18:4). Good news is like fresh water

Notes

(Proverbs 25:25). Several passages refer to our sins being washed away (Psalm 51:7; Ephesians 5:26; Hebrews 10:22).

Jesus told the Samaritan woman that he had water that would take away her thirst forever. The water he was speaking of was not, of course, two parts hydrogen and one part oxygen, but spiritual water—a water that will fill her so full of himself that all her needs would be met, all her wants satisfied, and all her thirst fulfilled.

The Woman of Samaria's Legacy in Scripture

Read John 4:7–9.

1. What makes it obvious that the Samaritan woman was surprised by Jesus' request?

2. This woman, an outcast because of her race and her lifestyle, found acceptance in Jesus. When have you associated with someone considered an outcast or befriended someone who wasn't part of your group?

Read John 4:10–18.

3. Do you think the woman understood what sort of water Jesus was speaking of here? Looking at her lifestyle, what do you think she was really thirsty for?

4. What have you used to try to fulfill your spiritual thirsts? Clothes? Family? Career? Recreation? Christ?

Read John 4:19–26.

5. The woman abruptly changes the subject in verse 19. Was she really interested in the answer or was she more interested in moving the topic away from her lifestyle?

6. Is it hard for you to face up to the areas of your life that need changing? What tactics do you use to keep the light of God's Word and Spirit away from your weaknesses and sins?

7. Verse 26 is the very first time Jesus acknowledges exactly who he is. Why do you think he would choose to tell this woman, an outcast of society, instead of the leaders of Jewish religion and culture or even his own disciples? Do you find his action delightful or just a bit distasteful?

Read John 4:27–42.

8. What one part of their conversation convinces the woman that Jesus was who he said he was?

9. What convinces you of the truth and validity of Jesus' claims? If you could meet him at a well, as this woman did, what would you ask him? What would convince you that he is what he says he is?

10. What does the Samaritan woman do when she realizes who Jesus is?

11. Once we've accepted the truth of Jesus' claims to be the Christ, what is the best response for us to make? How often do we actually respond in the way the Samaritan woman responded, and with as much enthusiasm?

40

The Woman
Who Lived
a Sinful Life

HER CHARACTER: She was a notorious sinner, possibly a prostitute or adultress. Rather than trying to defend what was indefensible in her life, she admitted her sin and made a spectacle of herself in a passionate display of love and gratitude.

KEY SCRIPTURE: Luke 7:36–50

Now one of the Pharisees [Simon] invited Jesus to have dinner with him, so he went to the Pharisee's house and reclined at the table. When a woman who had lived a sinful life in that town learned that Jesus was eating at the Pharisee's house, she brought an alabaster jar of perfume, and as she stood behind him at his feet weeping, she began to wet his feet with her tears. Then she wiped them with her hair, kissed them and poured perfume on them.

When the Pharisee who had invited him saw this, he said to himself, "If this man were a prophet, he would know who is touching him and what kind of woman she is—that she is a sinner."

. . . Then [Jesus] turned toward the woman and said to Simon, "Do you see this woman? I came into your house. You did not give me any water for my feet, but she wet my feet with her tears and wiped them with her hair. You did not give me a kiss, but this woman, from the time I entered, has not stopped kissing my feet. You did not put oil on my head, but she has poured perfume on my feet. Therefore, I tell you, her many sins have been forgiven— for she loved much. But he who has been forgiven little loves little."

LUKE 7:36–39, 44–47

The Sinful Woman's Life and Times

Washing Feet

The scene in this story is one of about thirteen instances in which Scripture talks about washing one's feet. The sinful woman in this story did the act reserved for the lowest, most inexperienced servant of the household.

Most people in Palestine wore sandals or went barefoot, so their feet were constantly dirty from the dust of the roads and fields. When they went into a house, they removed their sandals at the door. A good host or hostess made sure guests' feet were washed as soon as they entered the home. A basin of cool water and a towel were the only equipment required. After walking on hot dusty roads, the foot washing provided not only clean feet for entering a home but also a refreshing start to a visit.

When the three visitors came to Abraham when he was living "near the great trees of Mamre" (doesn't that sound like a wonderful place to live?), Abraham provided water for them to wash their feet (Genesis 18:1–5). Lot revealed the basic rules of Eastern hospitality when he invited the two angels into his home, telling them to "wash your feet and spend the night" (Genesis 19:1–3). Laban provided water for all of those with Abraham's servant to wash their feet (Genesis 24:32). In Egypt, Joseph made sure his brothers had water to wash their feet after their long journey from Palestine (Genesis 43:24). The priests were told they must always wash their feet and hands before going into the temple (Exodus 30:19–21). Not surprisingly, the list of good deeds that New Testament widows should be known for included, along with raising children and showing hospitality, "washing the feet of the saints" (1 Timothy 5:10).

The fact that foot washing was a task reserved for the lowest servant in the household makes Jesus' act of washing the disciples' feet (John 13) all the more poignant. His simple act shocked them and showed them in the clearest way possible how to be a servant leader. Washing. Touching feet fouled by dust and grime. *Kneeling* before those who by rights should kneel before him!

Our Life and Times

Not always so easy, is it? Those unpleasant, humble tasks that require little expertise and gain little notice. Scrubbing the kitchen floor at church. Washing the greasy hair of an elderly man who cannot do it for himself. Folding laundry. Tending sick children. What menial chore is on your list of things to do today? It's not the task itself that's important; it's what's in your heart while doing it. Will you accomplish it with thoughts that you were meant to do greater things? Or with a simple love for the one you serve?

The Sinful Woman's Legacy in Scripture

Read Luke 7:36–43.

1. What do you think the woman was looking for when she came to see Jesus at Simon's house? Attention? Forgiveness? An opportunity to express her love? Do you think everyone at the dinner knew who and what she was?

2. Describe what sort of feelings this woman might have had as she entered the house. When have you felt that way? Were you brave enough to continue like this woman did, or did you stop? Describe the situation and your actions.

3. Put this extravagant scene of verse 38 into your own words. Why do you think the woman acted this way?

4. How willing are you to be totally transparent in your worship? What would need to happen to make you as open in expressing your love for Jesus as this woman was?

5. Describe the Pharisee's attitude toward Jesus and toward the sinful woman.

6. Who are you more like: the judgmental Pharisee or the broken woman?

7. What did Jesus want Simon to understand from this story? Do you think he did?

8. In what ways can you be understanding and sympathetic toward those whose lives have been shattered by sin, like this woman? Toward those whose lives are characterized by judging others, like the Pharisee? Who needs forgiveness more?

9. Picture yourself as this sinful woman. Who has been like Jesus to you? Who has acted toward you like the Pharisee?

Read Luke 7:44–50.

10. In Luke 7:44–47 Jesus talks about this woman, using her as an example to teach something to Simon. What do you suppose she was thinking at this point?

11. Have you ever been made an example, good or bad, for others? How did you feel?

41

THE WOMAN WITH AN ISSUE OF BLOOD

HER CHARACTER: Desperate for healing, she ignored the conventions of the day just for the chance to touch Jesus.

KEY SCRIPTURES: Matthew 9:20–22; Mark 5:25–34; Luke 8:43–48

A large crowd followed and pressed around [Jesus]. And a woman was there who had been subject to bleeding for twelve years. She had suffered a great deal under the care of many doctors and had spent all she had, yet instead of getting better she grew worse. When she heard about Jesus, she came up behind him in the crowd and touched his cloak, because she thought, "If I just touch his clothes, I will be healed." Immediately her bleeding stopped and she felt in her body that she was freed from her suffering.

At once Jesus realized that power had gone out from him. He turned around in the crowd and asked, "Who touched my clothes?"

"You see the people crowding against you," his disciples answered, "and yet you can ask, 'Who touched me?'"

But Jesus kept looking around to see who had done it. Then the woman, knowing what had happened to her, came and fell at his feet and, trembling with fear, told him the whole truth. He said to her, "Daughter, your faith has healed you. Go in peace and be freed from your suffering."

MARK 5:24–34

The Sick Woman's Life and Times

Menstrual Bleeding

Any woman who has suffered through "an issue of blood" knows the difficulties and debilitating effects of the disease. When blood flows freely and frequently instead of in its regular monthly pattern, women endure not only the untidiness of the condition but can also experience a loss of strength and weight.

The woman in this story suffered from such a hemorrhage for twelve long years. She was probably weak and thin. Because of the ritual uncleanness that surrounded such a condition, she most likely didn't very often go out into public. Imagine twelve years of this:

> When a woman has a discharge of blood for many days at a time other than her monthly period or has a discharge that continues beyond her period, she will be unclean as long as she has the discharge, just as in the days of her period. Any bed she lies on while her discharge continues will be unclean, as is her bed during her monthly period, and anything she sits on will be unclean, as during her period. Whoever touches them will be unclean; he must wash his clothes and bathe with water, and he will be unclean till evening.
>
> LEVITICUS 15:25–27

A woman was considered unclean for a mere seven days when she had her regular period (Leviticus 15:19). This woman, however, bore not only the inconvenience but also the curse of being unclean for twelve years. Any*one* and any*thing* she touched became unclean. Imagine: she gives her husband a plate of food and their hands touch—he's unclean. She gives her neighbor a hand with her laundry and their hands touch—she's unclean. Anything she sits on at home becomes unclean, as does anything she sits on at a neighbor's home or in public. Before long, everyone is aware of her uncleanness and no one wants to be around her.

Many different female conditions could have caused this woman's ailment: fibroid tumors, an infection, a hormone imbalance. Whatever the cause, the doctors she had seen over the years had taken all of her money but given no relief. With the forthrightness and compassion that are characteristic of gospel writer Mark, he says this woman "had suffered a great deal under the care of many doctors." In fact, at times their cure was probably worse than her sickness. Still, no matter how much money she spent or how much agony she endured, her sickness seemed impossible to cure. Until she met the God of the impossible.

What doctors couldn't do, Jesus could. No repulsive or painful remedies. No visits to doctors more interested in financial gain than in her
cure. With just a soft, loving touch of his coat, she was cured. Healed.
Freed. Immediately!

Our Life and Times

The glory of Christ is that he succeeds where others fail. He brings healing when doctors say none is possible. He offers forgiveness when the
heart says it can never be forgiven. He extends comfort when the agony
is too great to carry and peace when all is chaos. He presented this sick
woman with the possible after twelve years of the impossible.

Notes

The Sick Woman's Legacy in Scripture

Read Mark 5:24–34.

1. Choose three words that best describe the kind of suffering experienced by this woman who had been bleeding for twelve long years.

2. Probably this woman accidentally touched others in the crowd when she was trying to get to Jesus. What do you think the crowd would have said or done if they had known she was sick and was unclean? What did it take for this woman to accept such a risk?

3. Mark says this woman was thinking, "If I just touch his clothes, I will be healed" (5:28). What does this tell you about this woman? How does this relate to Jesus' statement in verse 34 that her faith has healed her?

4. How do you think Jesus knew someone had touched him? Obviously, the touch of this woman was different from the other touches by those around him. What made it different?

5. Describe how you might feel if you had the opportunity to actually touch Jesus physically. Is there anything about this woman—her suffering, her actions, her healing—that reminds you of yourself? What is it?

6. Why do you think this woman was afraid to admit she was the one in the crowd who had touched Jesus and been healed (5:33)?

7. Think of a time when something very special or miraculous happened to you. Were you eager or hesitant to share it with others? Why?

8. Why does Jesus call this woman "daughter" (5:34)? How do you think the woman felt when Jesus spoke these words to her?

9. This woman had tried everything in order to be healed. When Jesus came to her village, she knew she had another option. How often do you try every other option to solve a problem before turning to God? Is he often a last resort for you? What would be a better way?

42

HERODIAS

Her Name, the Female Form of "Herod," Means "Heroic"

HER CHARACTER: A proud woman, she used her daughter to manipulate her husband into doing her will. She acted arrogantly, from beginning to end, in complete disregard for the laws of the land.

KEY SCRIPTURES: Matthew 14:3–12; Mark 6:14–29; Luke 3:19–20; 9:7–9

Now Herod had arrested John and bound him and put him in prison because of Herodias, his brother Philip's wife, for John had been saying to him: "It is not lawful for you to have her." Herod wanted to kill John, but he was afraid of the people, because they considered him a prophet.

On Herod's birthday the daughter of Herodias danced for them and pleased Herod so much that he promised with an oath to give her whatever she asked. Prompted by her mother, she said, "Give me here on a platter the head of John the Baptist." The king was distressed, but because of his oaths and his dinner guests, he ordered that her request be granted and had John beheaded in the prison. His head was brought in on a platter and given to the girl, who carried it to her mother. John's disciples came and took his body and buried it. Then they went and told Jesus.

———— MATTHEW 14:3–12 ————

Herodias's Life and Times

The Herods

Both husbands of Herodias were part of the Herodian family of rulers, as was Herodias herself. Her first husband, Herod Philip, as well as her second husband, Herod Antipas, were her uncles as well as her husbands. (For additional information on the family of the Herods, turn to the charts on pages 237–38.)

The family of the Herods ruled in Judea and the surrounding areas for over 125 years. The first Herod, known as Herod the Great, was king of Judea from 37 to 4 B.C. His reign was marked by division and domestic troubles, but also by prosperity. While in power, he built amphitheaters, palaces, fortresses, Gentile temples, and the Temple of Herod in Jerusalem. This temple was his crowning achievement, noted by the historian Josephus as Herod's most noble work. The literature of the rabbis of that time states: "He who has not seen the Temple of Herod has never seen a beautiful building."

Herod's five wives produced seven sons, most of whom went on to rule parts of the Near East for the Roman Empire. Herod's son by Mariamne of Simon, Philip, was Herodias's first husband. Herodias herself was a daughter of another of Herod's sons. That made her Herod's granddaughter as well as his daughter-in-law by marriage. Herodias wasn't the only one of Herod's children to form such relationships; Herod's great-granddaughter, Bernice, became the consort of her brother, Herod Agrippa II, also a great-grandchild of Herod.

The events at the birthday banquet described in Mark 6 are the culmination of years of corrupt living by a family who had power and knew how to use and misuse it. Herodias's actions, though horrifying, are not really surprising. Each step along the way to requesting John the Baptist's death was perhaps a small one, little noticed, but each step made its relentless way down a path to sin, until what would have been unconscionable years before now seemed acceptable and reasonable. Sin is like that. As your mother told you—and it's true—one small lie leads to another bigger lie that leads to another even bigger lie. The path of sin is strewn with small, seemingly insignificant decisions that lead nowhere but farther along the path away from truth and God.

Herodias's Legacy in Scripture

Read Mark 6:17–23.

1. Why do you think Herod had John put in prison? Because he wanted to please his wife or because he was angry and afraid of John himself?

2. When someone confronts you with something that is wrong in your life, how do you respond?

3. Note the different responses to John recorded in verses 19 and 20. What do these responses tell you about Herod and Herodias?

4. Which response is more like yours when confronted with sin? Are you like Herodias—sulking and wanting to get even with those who reveal your sin or failings? Or are you like Herod—willing to listen, curious about what the other person has to say?

5. What do you think Salome's dance must have been like to produce such an extravagant promise from her stepfather?

6. Have you ever promised something to someone that you later wished you hadn't? What did you do?

Read Mark 6:24–25.

7. Have you ever plotted, like Herodias, to get your own way? How does that make you feel about yourself? Are you pleased when you get your own way, or is the result less than satisfying?

Read Mark 6:26–29.

8. What other response could Herod have given? Was he obligated in some way to fulfill his promise, or could he have told her to come with another, more reasonable request?

9. When have you done something you later wished you hadn't simply because of the pressure of those around you to do it? What would have been a better response?

43

JOANNA

Her Name Means
"The Lord Gives Graciously"

HER CHARACTER: A woman of high rank in Herod's court, she experienced healing at Jesus' hands. She responded by giving herself totally, supporting his ministry and following him wherever he went. The story of her healing may have been known to Herod himself.

KEY SCRIPTURES: Luke 8:1–3; 24:10 (and Matthew 14:1–12 and Luke 23:7–12 for background on Herod and his court)

Notes

Jesus traveled about from one town and village to another, proclaiming the good news of the kingdom of God. The Twelve were with him, and also some women who had been cured of evil spirits and diseases: Mary (called Magdalene) from whom seven demons had come out; Joanna the wife of Cuza, the manager of Herod's household; Susanna; and many others. These women were helping to support them out of their own means. . . .

On the first day of the week, very early in the morning, the women took the spices they had prepared and went to the tomb. They found the stone rolled away from the tomb, but when they entered, they did not find the body of the Lord Jesus. While they were wondering about this, suddenly two men in clothes that gleamed like lightning stood beside them. In their fright the women bowed down with their faces to the ground, but the men said to them, "Why do you look for the living among the dead? He is not here; he has risen!"

LUKE 8:1–3; 24:1–6

Joanna's Life and Times

Healing

For most minor illnesses, ancient people depended on family members or neighbors who had some skill in the healing arts. A more severe illness would be treated by a priest who also acted as a physician. Since most disease was thought to be caused by spirits or demons, priest-physicians were appropriate healers. Medical practice focused heavily on spiritual remedies. Most Near Eastern people thought disease-causing spirits entered through the openings in the head. Some Egyptian physicians went so far as to drill holes in the patient's head in order to give the demons a means of escape.

The information in Scripture on disease has more to do with its prevention than its cure. When a patient recovered from a disease, regardless of the treatment that brought about healing, God was given credit. For instance, God is credited with the disappearance of Hezekiah's boil after it was treated with a poultice of figs (2 Kings 20:1–7).

One of Jesus' early healings was of a man suffering from the skin disease known as leprosy (Mark 1:40–42). People dreaded leprosy not only because of its destruction of skin and extremities but because it was thought to be contagious. Anyone with the disease was an outcast, unclean, separated from friends, family, and all that was familiar, with little or no hope for a cure. But then Jesus stepped into the picture. With only two words, "Be clean!" Jesus did what all the others had failed to do, and the man went away healed.

Joanna is listed with several other women whom Jesus had "cured of evil spirits and diseases." Scripture doesn't say exactly what her particular ailment was, but obviously it was something significant, something from which she had been unable to find relief through conventional methods. She and the other healed women now followed Jesus and supported him and his disciples.

No disease or deformity was beyond Jesus' healing power. He removed paralysis (Mark 2:3–12). He stopped bleeding (Mark 5:25–29). Those who were mute and blind could speak and see (Matthew 9:27–33; 20:29–34; Mark 8:22–26). Fevers left bodies at his touch (Mark 1:30–31). He restored shriveled limbs (Mark 3:1–5; Luke 13:11–13). Those possessed by evil spirits of one sort or another found relief and deliverance at Jesus' hands (Matthew 12:22; Mark 1:23–26; 9:17–29).

Our Life and Times

That same Jesus still heals today. Sometimes through the remarkable ability and knowledge of modern medicine and doctors. Sometimes without any human intervention. Sometimes by bringing the sick one home to heaven. Jesus' healing is always divine, if not miraculous. And his healing is always accompanied with his loving, all-pervasive touch.

Joanna's Legacy in Scripture

Read Luke 8:1–3.

1. What do you think this part of Jesus' ministry was like? Describe what you think his disciples may have done throughout the course of a day.

2. To whom do you minister in the course of your day? What people around you need the sort of ministry spoken of in this verse? Keep in mind that while Jesus was traveling and proclaiming the good news he was also healing the sick and "doing good" (Acts 10:38).

3. What sorts of diseases might Jesus have cured in these women? What was their response? Jesus healed many people, most of whom thanked him and praised God for their healing. But these women went beyond mere thanks to very practical acts of gratitude. Why do you think they responded this way?

4. Have you ever been healed of a sickness? Have you ever been saved from a life-threatening situation? Have you ever found relief from low spirits or evil spirits or depression? Who brought about your deliverance? What practical acts of gratitude can you, like Joanna and the other women, do in response?

Read Luke 24:1–10.

5. Joanna took care of Jesus during his life, supporting him with her work and her money. Now she is planning to take care of him in his death. What does she find instead?

6. Have you ever been totally surprised by a turn of events? Especially something that you thought was going to be terrible that turned out to be wonderful? What was your response?

Read Luke 24:11–12.

7. Why didn't the disciples believe what the women told them? Do you think if you had been there you would have thought it was "nonsense" also? What other reaction might you have had?

44

THE SYROPHOENICIAN WOMAN

HER CHARACTER: Though a Gentile, she addressed Jesus as "Lord, Son of David." Her great faith resulted in her daughter's deliverance.

KEY SCRIPTURES: Matthew 15:21–28; Mark 7:24–30

Jesus . . . went to the vicinity of Tyre. He entered a house and did not want anyone to know it; yet he could not keep his presence secret. In fact, as soon as she heard about him, a woman whose little daughter was possessed by an evil spirit came and fell at his feet. The woman was a Greek, born in Syrian Phoenicia. She begged Jesus to drive the demon out of her daughter.

"First let the children eat all they want," he told her, "for it is not right to take the children's bread and toss it to their dogs."

"Yes, Lord," she replied, "but even the dogs under the table eat the children's crumbs."

Then he told her, "For such a reply, you may go; the demon has left your daughter."

She went home and found her child lying on the bed, and the demon gone.

MARK 7:24–30

The Syrophoenician Woman's Life and Times

Demon-Possession

The New Testament teems with stories of people possessed by demons. Demons are fallen angels, emissaries of Satan, sent to earth to oppress human beings and lead them astray. Under Satan's control, their only goal is to further his purposes. They have supernatural powers here on earth: supernatural intelligence—they know and try to hide the truth (1 John 4:1–3) and they recognize Jesus as God's Son (Mark 5:7); and supernatural strength—a man possessed by demons could break away even when chained (Luke 8:29).

Though supernatural in their strength, demons are not more powerful than God or his Son. Whenever demons came face to face with Christ or his disciples in the New Testament, they trembled and did his bidding.

What the New Testament describes as demon-possessed people we would today depict as having an illness of some sort, physical or mental. How much distinction can be made between the two is uncertain. After Jesus cast a demon out of one man, he was described as "sitting there, dressed and in his right mind" (Mark 5:15). The man's demon-possession could easily have been extreme mental illness. At times, demon-possession caused muteness or blindness or convulsions (Matthew 9:32; 12:22; Mark 9:20). We can only speculate whether today we would view these illnesses as purely physical.

It is interesting to note that demons are mentioned only twice in the Old Testament (Deuteronomy 32:17; Psalm 106:37), yet over seventy times in the New Testament—all but a few of those in the Gospels. Perhaps Jesus' ministry to the sick exposed demonic activity as never before. Or perhaps Satan focused an extraordinary amount of his strength and power over the land of Israel while Jesus walked and healed there.

Our Life and Times

When Jesus left this earth, he sent the Holy Spirit to indwell his people. The life of Christ within us, as believers, is our defense against the forces of evil. We may suffer from physical, emotional, or mental illnesses that seem like demons within us, and God often uses the power of medical treatment to heal us of those illnesses—but let's not discount the power we possess within ourselves as children of God. That power forms a hedge of protection around and within us as we maintain a close relationship with God the Father, Christ his Son, and the Holy Spirit, our strength and comfort.

The Syrophoenician Woman's Legacy in Scripture

Read Matthew 15:21–28.

1. What about the words in verse 22 makes it obvious that this woman and her daughter were both suffering?

2. If your child were the one possessed, how would you approach Jesus for healing? What would you say? How would you act?

3. Why do you suppose Jesus at first ignored the woman? What was her response?

4. Was it okay for this woman to keep "crying out"? Why or why not?

5. This woman was not an Israelite. What might have been her response to Jesus' statement that he had come "only to the lost sheep of Israel"? Why do you think she didn't give up?

6. How persistent are you in prayer? Do you give up easily? Or do you keep praying until you get a definite answer?

7. What was meant by the "crumbs" in verse 27? What was this woman saying?

8. What was Jesus' response? Why did he respond in the way he did?

9. When have you asked for little and received much? Were you surprised? How often do we settle for the "crumbs" when Jesus really wants to give us the whole loaf?

Read Matthew 15:23, 28.

10. What is the difference between how the disciples responded to the woman and how Jesus ultimately responded to her?

11. When a needy person approaches you, do you respond like Jesus or like his disciples? How do you respond if the person is *emotionally* needy—continually sticking close to you, interrupting your conversations with others, asking questions you can't answer, and generally wanting more than you wish to give?

MARTHA

*Her Name, the Feminine Form
of "Lord," Means "Lady"*

HER CHARACTER: Active and pragmatic, she seemed never at a loss for words. Though Jesus chastened her for allowing herself to become worried and upset by small things, she remained his close friend and follower.

KEY SCRIPTURES: Luke 10:38–42; John 11:1–12:3

᙮

As Jesus and his disciples were on their way, he came to a village where a woman named Martha opened her home to him. She had a sister called Mary, who sat at the Lord's feet listening to what he said. But Martha was distracted by all the preparations that had to be made. She came to him and asked, "Lord, don't you care that my sister has left me to do the work by myself? Tell her to help me!"

"Martha, Martha," the Lord answered, "you are worried and upset about many things, but only one thing is needed. Mary has chosen what is better, and it will not be taken away from her."

LUKE 10:38–42

Martha's Life and Times

Women's Work

The work expected of a woman in Bible times was much more clearly defined than it is in our culture. There were things the women did and things the men did; things the female children did and things the male children did.

Martha was just doing what she thought was expected of her. She had been raised to take care of her guests, to care for the people in her household. *Mary* was the one who stepped outside of the cultural expectations of her time, sitting at the feet of Jesus with the men rather than working with Martha in the kitchen. When Martha complained, Jesus responded with characteristic boldness, ignoring the dictates of his time and urging Martha to stop and consider the choice Mary had made.

Women of that time kept busy from morning to evening with a daunting array of household tasks:

- grinding grain for bread, then mixing, kneading, and baking the bread for the day
- purchasing meat at a market or preparing an animal from the household's flock for meat to eat, then cooking that meat
- carding, spinning, and weaving threads of various kinds to make cloth for clothing, bedding, and other household uses
- sewing clothing for household members
- drawing the water for each day's requirements
- cleaning the house
- washing the utensils and dishes used in meal preparation and eating
- washing the family's clothing
- teaching and disciplining and loving the children in the household

Our Life and Times

The list could go on and on, and it is not so very different from the lists many women today could make of their responsibilities as wives and mothers. The tasks may be overwhelming. They may seem tedious and exhausting. But they are never unimportant.

Jesus' words to Martha should not be construed to mean that "women's work" should be ignored and left undone. That would be unrealistic. However, such work should never take the place of daily and intimate contact with the members of our families and the Lord of our lives.

Martha's Legacy in Scripture

Read Luke 10:38–42.

1. What do the words "opened her home" (10:38) tell you about Martha?

2. When have you opened your home to someone? Not just had them over for coffee or a meal, but let them use your home as their own? Opened your heart to them as well as your home? Describe the person and the circumstances.

3. Hospitality is listed as a gift in 1 Peter 4:9. Do you have the gift of hospitality? How do you use it?

4. Describe what you think the scene in verse 39 looked like.

5. Compare Mary and Martha. Which woman are you more like?

6. Often, this story puts Martha in a negative light and Mary in a positive one. Do you think that's fair? Why or why not?

7. Martha was frank with Jesus. What does that tell you about her relationship with him? Why do you think she complained to Jesus instead of going directly to Mary?

8. If you were honest with Jesus, more honest than you've ever been before, what would you say to him?

9. What was Jesus trying to tell Martha?

10. If Jesus were to come to visit you today, would you busy yourself with preparations, as Martha did, or sit at his feet, like Mary? Which position would you be most comfortable with?

11. What in your life would Jesus think is a distraction from spending more time with him? Would he think these distractions were any more legitimate than Martha's?

Read John 11:27.

12. We often study Martha and see her shortcomings. However, this statement, made after her brother, Lazarus, had died, reveals another side of Martha. What does her declaration here tell you about who Martha really was?

46

MARY OF BETHANY

Her Name May Mean "Bitterness"

Notes

HER CHARACTER: Mary appears to have been a single woman, totally devoted to Jesus. The gospel portrays her, by way of contrast with her sister, Martha, as a woman of few words. As Jesus neared the time of his triumphal entry into Jerusalem prior to Passover, she performed a gesture of great prophetic significance, one that offended Judas Iscariot, the disciple who betrayed Jesus.

KEY SCRIPTURES: Matthew 26:6–13; Mark 14:3–9; Luke 10:38–42; John 11:1–12:11

Now a man named Lazarus was sick. He was from Bethany, the village of Mary and her sister Martha. . . . So the sisters sent word to Jesus, "Lord, the one you love is sick."

On his arrival, Jesus found that Lazarus had already been in the tomb for four days. . . .

"Take away the stone," he said. . . .

So they took away the stone. Then Jesus . . . called in a loud voice, "Lazarus, come out!" The dead man came out. . . .

Jesus said to them, "Take off the grave clothes and let him go." . . .

Six days before the Passover, Jesus arrived at Bethany. . . . Here a dinner was given in Jesus' honor. Martha served, while Lazarus was among those reclining at the table with him. Then Mary took about a pint of pure nard, an expensive perfume; she poured it on Jesus' feet and wiped his feet with her hair. And the house was filled with the fragrance of the perfume.

JOHN 11:1, 3, 17, 39, 41, 43–44; 12:1–3

Mary's Life and Times

The Passover

All able-bodied and ceremonially clean Jewish men, usually accompanied by their families, were required to attend Passover in Jerusalem as well as two other major religious feasts, Pentecost and Tabernacles (Exodus 23:17), throughout the year.

The Feast of Passover took place in Nisan, the first month of the ancient Jewish year, our April. (For a chart of the Jewish calendar, turn to page 233.) The most significant feast celebrated by the Jews, Passover commemorated their deliverance from slavery in Egypt. At that time, Moses had commanded each family to kill an unblemished one-year-old male lamb. He had instructed them to take the blood from the lamb and, using a brush made of hyssop branches, spread the blood on the sides and top of the doorframe of each household. When the tenth and last plague came to Egypt, the angel of death entered only those houses without blood on the doorpost and killed the firstborn son in each family. Any home with blood on the doorway was "passed over."

Jewish families ate the meat of the lamb for their Passover supper, sharing with neighbors if the family was too small to finish the lamb alone. The meal also included a salad of bitter herbs as well as unleavened, or unrisen, bread. Before Passover, the house was thoroughly searched and cleaned to be sure no yeast was in the house to spoil the unleavened bread. This bread reminded the Jews of the haste with which they had to eat their last meal in Egypt before leaving slavery there. Psalms 113–118, known as the "Egyptian Hallel" (or Praise) psalms, were sung before and after the meal.

Often during their history, the Jews neglected to celebrate the Passover, as well as many of the other religious feasts God had instituted. The times when the Passover was reinstated are mentioned specifically in the Old Testament, and the ignorance of the people regarding the sacred nature of the feast is apparent. Most often, the restoration of the feast came about because of a religious revival (2 Kings 23:21–23; 2 Chronicles 30:1; 35:1–19; Ezra 6:19–22).

The Last Supper Jesus ate with his disciples, on the night that he was betrayed, was the annual Passover meal. Jesus gave specific instructions to several of his disciples for preparing this important meal. While he and his disciples reclined at the table, Jesus revealed that one of the Twelve would betray him and that he would be crucified.

Notes

Our Life and Times

With his words, "This is my body" and "This is my blood," Jesus gave new meaning and significance to the Passover lamb. When he was crucified the next day, he himself became our Passover Lamb. Though we may observe the beauty of the Passover, for believers, the work is done. Jesus' death on the cross as the ultimate Passover lamb made the continual sacrifice for sin no long necessary. Through his body and blood—through his work as our Passover lamb—we gain forgiveness for our sins and life eternal.

Mary's Legacy in Scripture

Read John 11:32–44.

1. Why is Mary crying here (11:32–33)? How does Jesus react to her grief?

2. Put yourself in Mary's place in this scene. Your brother, who lives with you and supports you, has died and then is raised. No information is given on the reactions of the sisters or the crowd. How do you think they reacted? How would you react?

3. Have you ever had something that caused you grief suddenly change to joy? A sickness healed? A child returned? How did you react? Whom did you thank?

Read John 12:1–8.

4. What do you think caused Mary to make the extravagant gesture described in verse 3?

5. If you were to take a year's worth of your wages (see John 12:5), what would you do with it for Jesus?

6. We're told exactly why this use of expensive perfume bothered Judas so much (12:5–6). What word best describes him here?

7. How sincere are you? Like Mary? Like Judas? Somewhere in between? If Jesus came to your house for dinner, what would you do to express your love for him?

8. Do you think Mary had any idea that this act of devotion was preparation for Jesus' burial? How do you think she might have reacted to his statement?

9. Did Jesus' words in verse 8 mean we should ignore the poor and pay attention only to him? If not, what exactly did he mean?

10. The poor are among us yet today, and so is Jesus, through the Holy Spirit. What can we do to help the poor? What can we do to acknowledge Jesus' presence in our world?

47

SALOME, MOTHER OF THE ZEBEDEES

Her Name, the Feminine Form of "Solomon," Means "Peace"

Notes

HER CHARACTER: The mother of two disciples of Jesus and the wife of a prosperous fisherman, Salome was herself a devoted follower of Jesus. But she shared the common misconception that the Messiah would drive out the Romans and establish a literal kingdom in Palestine.

KEY SCRIPTURES: Matthew 20:20–24; 27:56; Mark 15:40–41; 16:1–2

ʒ

Then the mother of Zebedee's sons came to Jesus with her sons and, kneeling down, asked a favor of him.

"What is it you want?" he asked.

She said, "Grant that one of these two sons of mine may sit at your right and the other at your left in your kingdom."

"You don't know what you are asking," Jesus said to them. "Can you drink the cup I am going to drink?"

"We can," they answered.

Jesus said to them, "You will indeed drink from my cup, but to sit at my right or left is not for me to grant. These places belong to those for whom they have been prepared by my Father."

—————— MATTHEW 20:20–23 ——————

Salome's Life and Times

M o t h e r i n g

In biblical times, when a man married, he gained another possession. Every wife was under her husband's absolute authority. When a man decided "to marry a wife," the meaning of the phrase was closer to "become the master of a wife." But even though a woman's position in the household was one of subservience to her husband, she was still in a higher position than anyone else in the household.

A woman's principal duty was to produce a family, preferably sons, who could ensure the family's financial future. Mothers generally nursed their youngsters until they were about three years old. During that time, husbands and wives did not usually engage in sexual intercourse, a natural form of birth control that gave the mother time to devote herself to her youngest child.

Mothers had total care of their children, both sons and daughters, until they were about six years old. The children helped their mother with household tasks, and she taught them basic lessons on living in their culture. After six years of age, most boys became the family shepherd or began to spend the day with their father, learning the family business. David, as the youngest son, took care of his family's sheep and goats (1 Samuel 16:11), and Jesus probably spent time with his father Joseph learning his carpentry trade (Mark 6:3). Daughters stayed with their mothers throughout their growing-up years. Mothers taught their daughters spinning and weaving and cooking, as well as how to behave and what to expect in their future roles as wives and mothers.

Gradually the role of mothers came to include activities like those described in Proverbs 31. Throughout Scripture, the role of mothering is given dignity and significance, so much so that God describes his love for us as his children in terms of mothering. "As a mother comforts her child, so will I [the Lord] comfort you" (Isaiah 66:13). Paul describes his care for the Thessalonians as the care of a mother for her children: "We were gentle among you, like a mother caring for her little children" (1 Thessalonians 2:7).

Our Life and Times

When you find yourself lost in the chaos and clutter of caring for young children, remember the important part you play in keeping their world safe and happy. When you find yourself buried in the mess and muddle of raising elementary school children, remember how much they rely on you for their security. When you find yourself struggling with the disaster and disarray of raising teenagers, remember how much you love them and how much they need you to believe in them. Never forget: If you have children, they are one of your greatest legacies.

Salome's Legacy in Scripture

Read Matthew 20:20–28.

1. What did James's and John's mother really want? Do you think she was asking only for honor for her sons, or did she also want something for herself?

2. How do you react when your child is honored? How do you react when your child is passed over for some honor? How are you like Salome?

3. What "cup" is Jesus talking about in verse 22? Do you think the disciples answered his question glibly or seriously?

4. Would it be wise to prevent all suffering in the lives of your children? Why or why not?

5. Why were the other disciples upset with James and John instead of with James's and John's mother? Do you think James and John had some part in their mother's actions?

6. If you had been there, what would you have said to Salome? Have you ever said something similar to the mother of one of your child's friends, perhaps not to her face but at least to yourself? Why are mothers so eager to protect and elevate their own children?

7. With the words of verses 26–28, Jesus totally overturns the natural reactions of his culture and ours. How do you think the disciples and Salome reacted to his words? What do you think Salome might have been thinking at this point?

8. How easy or hard is it for you to play the role of servant? Define servant leadership. What has to change in your life for you to truly become a servant leader?

48

THE WIDOW
WITH TWO COINS

HER CHARACTER: Though extremely poor, she is one of the most great-hearted people in the Bible. Just after warning his disciples to watch out for the teachers of the law, who devour widows' houses, Jesus caught sight of her in the temple. He may have called attention to her as a case in point.

KEY SCRIPTURES: Mark 12:41–44; Luke 21:1–4

Notes

Jesus sat down opposite the place where the offerings were put and watched the crowd putting their money into the temple treasury. Many rich people threw in large amounts. But a poor widow came and put in two very small copper coins, worth only a fraction of a penny.

Calling his disciples to him, Jesus said, "I tell you the truth, this poor widow has put more into the treasury than all the others. They all gave out of their wealth; but she, out of her poverty, put in everything—all she had to live on."

MARK 12:41–44

The Widow's Life and Times

Money

Two tiny coins. Mark identifies them as two Greek lepta, tiny copper coins worth less than a penny.

Roman coins (*denarius*), Greek coins (*drachma, farthing*), and Jewish coins (*mite, pound, shekel,* and *talent*) are all mentioned in the New Testament. (For more information on money in ancient times, turn to page 236.) The Israelites typically used the coinage of the nation that ruled over them, but they also developed their own local system of coinage.

Coins didn't actually come into use in Israel until after the people returned from exile between 500 and 400 B.C. Before that time people bartered, exchanging produce, animals, and precious metals for goods and services. A woman might barter a flask of oil for a new robe or the wool from a lamb for a new lamp.

The Israelites probably carried Persian and Babylonian coins back to Israel with them when they returned from exile there. These coins were rather crudely made. Each was individually punched from gold or silver or some other metal, then a design was hammered onto each side. Greek coins most often had images of nature or animals or gods stamped onto them. Later, Roman coins carried the image of the emperor of that time, as well as his name. Coins have been found with the images of all twelve Roman emperors.

By Jesus' day, a large variety of coins had come into use in Palestine. New Testament Jews used coins from Rome and Greece as well as their own Jewish form of coinage. The temple tax had to be paid in Jewish currency—in shekels. Money changers set up their businesses in order to change other coinage into shekels for temple worshipers. Jesus was not opposed to the operation of such businesses, but to their operation within the temple itself. He furiously scattered them, declaring that his Father's house was a house of prayer, not a business site (Matthew 21:12–13).

While money is necessary for life in most cultures, the Bible warns against placing more importance on it than it should rightfully have. The widow who gave all she had furnishes us with the best example of recognizing the need for money—she had money, although very little—but also the need to hold it lightly—she willingly and lovingly gave it away. Peter warns us not to be "greedy for money" (1 Peter 5:2), and the writer to the Hebrews admonishes us to keep our "lives free from the love of money and be content with what [we] have" (Hebrews 13:5). When writing to Timothy, Paul penned those famous, and often misquoted, words about money: "For the love of money is a root of all kinds of evil. Some people, eager for money, have wandered from the faith and pierced themselves with many griefs" (1 Timothy 6:10). A lover of money would have hung onto it more tightly than the widow and, when giving it away, would have made sure the gift was noisily apparent.

Our Life and Times

The pervasive lure of money and what it can provide—the need to have more and do more and get more—is probably more prevalent in our culture than in any other in history. Christians are just as susceptible to its enticements as anyone else. Money drives an effective and forceful wedge between our Savior and us. Jesus knew that, and pointedly reminded us of money's power with these words: "No servant can serve two masters. Either he will hate the one and love the other, or he will be devoted to the one and despise the other. You cannot serve both God and Money" (Luke 16:13).

The Widow's Legacy in Scripture

Read Mark 12:41–44.

1. Why would Jesus watch people putting money into the offering? What do you think he was looking for?

2. Picture yourself in this scene: You're in the temple, putting your offering into the receptacle. You don't know it, but Jesus is watching. What does he see?

3. The trumpet-shaped receptacles for offerings were made of metal. Compare the difference between the sound of the widow's offering with the sound of the offerings of the rich. Who do you think was most noticed by the crowd? Who did Jesus notice?

4. What did Jesus see about the woman that others in the crowd missed? What might Jesus see about you that others around you might miss?

5. What was significant about the widow's offering? Why do you think Jesus pointed the widow's offering out to his disciples? What did he want them to think, to understand?

6. How does the widow's offering compare to the offering Jesus was about to make? What was similar about it? What was different?

7. In one sentence, summarize what the Holy Spirit is teaching you through this story.

49

MARY MAGDALENE

Her Name May Mean "Bitterness"

HER CHARACTER: Though mistakenly characterized as a prostitute in many popular writings, the Bible says only that Mary was possessed by seven demons. She probably suffered a serious mental or physical illness from which Jesus delivered her. She is a beautiful example of a woman whose life was poured out in response to God's extravagant grace.

KEY SCRIPTURES: Matthew 27:56, 61; 28:1; Mark 15:40, 47; 16:1–19; Luke 8:2; 24:10; John 19:25; 20:1–18

Notes

While it was still dark, Mary Magdalene went to the tomb and saw that the stone had been removed from the entrance....

Mary stood outside the tomb crying. As she wept, she bent over to look into the tomb and saw two angels. . . . They asked her, "Woman, why are you crying?"

"They have taken my Lord away," she said, "and I don't know where they have put him." At this, she turned around and saw Jesus standing there, but she did not realize that it was Jesus.

"Woman," he said, "why are you crying? Who is it you are looking for?"

Thinking he was the gardener, she said, "Sir, if you have carried him away, tell me where you have put him, and I will get him."

Jesus said to her, "Mary."

She turned toward him and cried out in Aramaic, "Rabboni!" (which means Teacher).

JOHN 20:1, 11–16

Mary Magdalene's Life and Times

Women in Jesus' Life and Ministry

Cooking, caring for family members, spinning, weaving, sewing, baking bread, cleaning—all of these were common tasks for women in New Testament times. Most women spent the majority of their time and energy within their homes, caring for their families. But several women stepped outside the cultural expectations of their time to play a significant role in the ministry of Jesus. Only the twelve disciples are mentioned more often than certain women, Mary Magdalene being one of them.

Mark tells us that a number of women "followed him [Jesus] and cared for his needs" (Mark 15:41). During the years of Jesus' ministry, when he and his disciples weren't earning an income, several women stepped in to care for them. They used their own financial resources to support Jesus and the disciples (Luke 8:3). While Jesus was teaching and healing, these women probably spent their time purchasing food, preparing it, and serving it. Perhaps they also found homes for Jesus and his disciples to stay in while on their travels. These particular women probably either didn't have children or had children who were grown, so their responsibilities at home were decreased, and they could instead provide for the needs of Jesus and his disciples.

Two women in Bethany, Mary and Martha, always generously opened their home to Jesus when he was in their town, providing meals and a place to rest (Luke 10:38). Jesus was close enough to these women and their brother, Lazarus, that he called them his friends (John 11:11).

The most significant woman in Jesus' life was, of course, Mary, his mother. She remained in the background during his years of public ministry, perhaps caring for younger children or grandchildren. Jesus' gentle care of her when he was hanging on the cross reveals a true son's love for his mother.

Women watched Jesus suffer on the cross, remaining there until he had breathed his last and was buried. Women were the first to go to the tomb on Sunday morning and the first to witness the Resurrection.

Our Life and Times

Luke's gospel in particular portrays Jesus as someone who both understood and respected women, conferring on them a stature that most of them had not previously enjoyed. Jesus' dealings with women throughout the Gospels gives all of us, men and women alike, a model to follow as we consider the status and treatment of the women with whom we come into contact every day.

Mary Magdalene's Legacy in Scripture

Read Mark 15:33–47.

1. Why do you think these women went and watched Jesus die on the cross? What drew them? Imagine, if you can, how they reacted when they saw he was dead.

2. Would you have gone to the cross? Would you have watched "from a distance" (15:40) or stayed at home? Try to imagine yourself there. Does this image change anything about what you feel for Jesus?

3. What do you think these women might have done for Jesus? How do you think they "cared for his needs" (15:41)? Why would all of these women follow Jesus to Jerusalem? What do you think they saw in Jesus that they didn't see in other men?

4. It is very likely that these women knew following Jesus to Jerusalem could be dangerous, but they went anyway. Would you still follow Jesus anywhere if it meant danger to you or to your family?

5. Why were the two Marys interested in where Jesus was buried? What might they have been planning to do?

6. Again, put yourself as a woman in this event. Would you have followed all the way to Jesus' tomb? What might you have been feeling besides grief?

Read John 20:1–16.

7. What did Mary think had happened to Jesus? Why was Jesus' resurrection so hard for them to believe?

8. Would Jesus' resurrection from the dead have been hard for you to believe? Why or why not?

9. Why do you think Mary didn't recognize Jesus? What made her recognize him? Why would Jesus' speaking her name make her know it was really him?

10. Do you think God knows you by name? If you're not sure, read Isaiah 43:1.

50

DORCAS

Her Name Means "Gazelle"
"Tabitha" Is Its Hebrew Equivalent

HER CHARACTER: An inhabitant of Joppa, a town on the Mediterranean coast thirty-five miles northwest of Jerusalem, she belonged to one of the earliest Christian congregations. She was a disciple known for her practical works of mercy.

KEY SCRIPTURE: Acts 9:36–43

Notes

In Joppa there was a disciple named Tabitha (which, when translated, is Dorcas), who was always doing good and helping the poor. About that time she became sick and died, and her body was washed and placed in an upstairs room. Lydda was near Joppa; so when the disciples heard that Peter was in Lydda, they sent two men to him and urged him, "Please come at once!"

Peter went with them, and when he arrived he was taken upstairs to the room. All the widows stood around him, crying and showing him the robes and other clothing that Dorcas had made while she was still with them.

Peter sent them all out of the room; then he got down on his knees and prayed. Turning toward the dead woman, he said, "Tabitha, get up." She opened her eyes, and seeing Peter she sat up. He took her by the hand and helped her to her feet. Then he called the believers and the widows and presented her to them alive.

—— ACTS 9:36–41 ——

Dorcas's Life and Times

Disciples

In Joppa there was a disciple named Tabitha (which, when translated, is Dorcas)" (Acts 9:36). Tabitha, or Dorcas, is the only woman in Scripture to be honored with the designation of disciple. The presence of women in groups of disciples is implied at times, but Dorcas is the only woman specifically called a disciple.

The word *disciple* has its roots in verbs that mean "to learn" or "to follow." Those two verbs describe the activity or posture of the disciple of the New Testament. The word *disciple* is used 284 times in the Bible. Two of those times occur in Isaiah, and all of the rest are found in the Gospels and in the book of Acts. The Scriptures use the word almost exclusively to name someone who is a follower of Jesus.

A disciple is first of all a learner, a pupil. The disciples of Jesus sat at his feet, and he taught them. They listened and soaked up the knowledge and wisdom of Christ as he talked to them and to the crowds that inevitably gathered around. Jesus taught them many things, but all of his teaching can be summed up in his command to love God and love others (Mark 12:31). As disciples, they accepted what Jesus taught as truth, trusting him as their teacher and willingly putting into practice all of his teachings.

Second, a disciple is a follower. The disciples followed Jesus wherever he went. Jesus' first words to Peter and his brother Simon were "Follow me." When Jesus called to James and John in their boat, they quickly left the boat and their father and followed Jesus (Matthew 4:18–22). The word *following* here doesn't just mean being willing to walk along with the teacher; it means being willing to adopt the views and way of life of the teacher. The twelve disciples left their families and incomes and former lifestyles to follow Jesus.

A true disciple, Dorcas had learned of Jesus and had decided to follow him. She had adopted his views and lifestyle, lovingly living out his commands by ministering to the poor around her. There was no mistaking it, no quibbling, no uncertainty—anyone who knew Dorcas knew who she was and whom she followed. Her devotion is recorded for all the generations to follow with those simple, yet profound words: "In Joppa there was a disciple named Tabitha."

Our Life and Times

If someone were to record our lives in just a few words, what words do you think they would choose? What a lofty goal we can have, to live as simply and as single-mindedly for Jesus as Dorcas did. Then, perhaps, the words that would describe our lives would be "In _____ there was a disciple named _____."

Dorcas's Legacy in Scripture

Read Acts 9:36–41.

1. Describe what sorts of things you think Dorcas was probably doing (9:36). Compare this verse with Acts 10:38.

2. Why do you think the disciples of Joppa wanted Peter to come? What picture does this verse give of Dorcas's activities for the poor? Who does it appear she especially helped?

3. The help Dorcas provided was an essential part of her character. She had the gift of helping. Even if you don't have that particular gift, are there ways that you can reach out to the needy, helping to meet their needs on your own or through your church or community?

4. Describe what you think the scene was like when Peter brought Dorcas back to her friends and neighbors.

5. Have you ever experienced such an event? What were the circumstances? How did you feel?

Read Acts 9:42.

6. What sort of response did people have to Dorcas's miracle?

7. God was definitely glorified through Dorcas's life, death, and resurrection. What if Dorcas had not been raised? Would God still have been glorified? How?

51

LYDIA

*Her Name Signifies That She Was a Woman
of Lydia, a Region in Asia Minor*

HER CHARACTER: A Gentile adherent of Judaism, she was a successful businesswoman who sold a type of cloth prized for its purple color. As head of her household, she may have been either widowed or single. So strong was her faith that her entire household followed her example and was baptized. She extended hospitality to Paul and his companions, even after their imprisonment.

KEY SCRIPTURE: Acts 16:6–40

Notes

᚛

[Luke wrote:] *We traveled to Philippi, a Roman colony and the leading city of that district of Macedonia. And we stayed there several days.*

On the Sabbath we went outside the city gate to the river, where we expected to find a place of prayer. We sat down and began to speak to the women who had gathered there. One of those listening was a woman named Lydia, a dealer in purple cloth from the city of Thyatira, who was a worshiper of God. The Lord opened her heart to respond to Paul's message. When she and the members of her household were baptized, she invited us to her home. "If you consider me a believer in the Lord," she said, "come and stay at my house." And she persuaded us.

———— ACTS 16:12–15 ————

Lydia's Life and Times

Fabrics and Dyes

Lydia's success as a businesswoman in the city of Philippi came from dealing in cloth that had been dyed a particular shade of purple. Originally from Thyatira, Lydia was probably privy to secret formulas for the dyes made there. Only those who belonged to the dyers' guild were allowed to work as dyers. Made from the secretions of a shellfish found in the area, these special dyes colored the clothing of the well-to-do. The particular shades of purple ranged from a reddish scarlet to a deep purple tone.

Cloth dyed in various colors is mentioned as early as the Exodus from Egypt, when the Lord instructed Moses to receive gifts from the people of Israel in order to make the tabernacle: "These are the offerings you are to receive from them: gold, silver and bronze; blue, purple and scarlet yarn and fine linen; goat hair; ram skins dyed red. . ." (Exodus 25:3–5).

The best red or scarlet dyes were made from a grub that fed on oak as well as other plants. A less expensive form of red dye could be made from the root of the madder plant. The rind of the pomegranate formed the basis for dyes of blue shades. Yellow dyes were made from safflower and turmeric.

The most common garments in biblical times were made from wool, which came naturally in a variety of colors, from whites and yellows to tans and browns. Wool was also easily dyed other colors. Linen fabric was more difficult to dye but was used in early Egypt (Genesis 41:42) and was used in making the tabernacle curtains (Exodus 26). Leathers for girdles, shields, sandals, purses, or pouches could also be dyed numerous colors.

Lydia's occupation, then, was an important commercial trade. She must have been at least moderately successful, for Scripture records the fact that she had her own house, as well as servants. Her unique position as a woman in business gave her opportunity to travel, to learn of the Christ, and to offer her home and hospitality to Paul and his companions as ministers of the gospel.

Our Life and Times

Lydia's mind and heart weren't consumed with her business. Her mind and heart were consumed with following God—in her business and outside of it. Lydia provides a remarkable example for today's businesswoman of one who was not only successful but also a servant.

Lydia's Legacy in Scripture

Read Acts 16:11–13.

1. In ancient times, when there was no synagogue in a city, it was the custom of those who worshiped the true God to gather for prayer outdoors, preferably near running water. Describe the scene created in your mind when you read verse 13.

2. What is your place of community worship like? Where do you think your community would gather for worship if you had no church building?

Read Acts 16:14–15.

3. What does the first part of verse 14 tell you about Lydia? Which of the things you know about Lydia from these few words would you consider most important?

4. Try to construct a sentence about yourself similar to this one about Lydia. Which of the things you list about yourself do you consider your most important characteristic?

5. What do you think is meant by the words, "The Lord opened her heart to respond" (16:14b)? If you have experienced something similar, what were the circumstances and what was your response?

6. Lydia responds to the gospel message with two actions (16:15). What are they?

7. How did she persuade Paul and his companions to stay at her house? Why do you think she was so anxious for them to stay with her?

Read Acts 16:40.

8. When Paul and Silas got out of prison, they immediately went to Lydia's home again. What does this verse say they did there? They had been beaten severely (verse 23) and put in stocks in prison (verse 24); however, they responded not by complaining or moaning over their circumstances but by encouraging the believers in Philippi. How do you think Lydia and her fellow believers responded to what Paul and Silas had to say to them?

9. It can be difficult to minister to others when your own problems and troubles are overwhelming. How can you be an encouragement to those around you in spite of your own trials? More than that, how can you be an encouragement to those around you *because of* your trials?

52

PRISCILLA

Her Name, the Diminutive of "Prisca,"
Means "Worthy" or "Venerable"

HER CHARACTER: One of the first missionaries and a leader of the early church, along with her husband, Aquila, she risked her life for the apostle Paul. Priscilla was a woman whose spiritual maturity and understanding of the faith helped build up the early church.

KEY SCRIPTURES: Acts 18–19; Romans 16:3–4; 1 Corinthians 16:19; 2 Timothy 4:19

Notes

[In Corinth Paul] met a Jew named Aquila, a native of Pontus, who had recently come from Italy with his wife Priscilla, because Claudius had ordered all the Jews to leave Rome. Paul went to see them, and because he was a tentmaker as they were, he stayed and worked with them. Every Sabbath he reasoned in the synagogue, trying to persuade Jews and Greeks. . . .

Apollos . . . was a learned man, with a thorough knowledge of the Scriptures. He had been instructed in the way of the Lord, and he spoke with great fervor and taught about Jesus accurately, though he knew only the baptism of John. He began to speak boldly in the synagogue. When Priscilla and Aquila heard him, they invited him to their home and explained to him the way of God more adequately.

ACTS 18:2–4, 24–26

Priscilla's Life and Times

Tentmaking

Although tents themselves are often mentioned in the Bible, the skill of tentmaking is only mentioned once, here in Acts 18. Paul stayed with Aquila and Priscilla and worked with them in their tentmaking trade.

By New Testament times the Israelites had settled in towns and cities. They no longer lived a nomadic lifestyle, moving their tents from place to place. However, traders and travelers still used these tents, and some Near Eastern desert peoples still lived in them. Indeed, some desert peoples today still live in tents similar to the ones Paul probably made.

Tents of the time were made of strong cloth woven of goat hair. Lengths of the cloth were sewn together to form tents that were sometimes round and sloping, sometimes oblong. Poles held the tent up, along with ropes that were stretched to stakes, which were driven into the ground to hold the poles and the cloth firmly in place. Mats of papyrus or more goat hair formed side curtains and interior walls to divide the people from each other or from their animals.

Paul was originally from Tarsus, a major city of Cilicia, a province known for its production of superior cloth made of goat hair. Jewish parents took seriously the responsibility of teaching their sons a trade, and Paul's parents were no exception. Paul learned the tentmaking trade and used it at times to support himself during his years of ministry.

As a tentmaker, Paul's skill probably was not so much in weaving the heavy cloth of goat hair but in measuring and cutting the lengths of cloth to the proper lengths and then sewing them together to form the tent itself. He would also have attached the ropes and loops necessary for the poles and stakes that held the tent in place.

We usually think of Paul in terms of his great missionary adventures. Seldom do we think of him in terms of a trade that involved working not with his quick and able mind so much as with his hands. More than anything, Paul's work as a tentmaker reveals to us the sacred nature of all work, whether esteemed or not by our culture.

Our Life and Times

All work is valuable and worthwhile in God's sight, and all work is worth doing "with all your heart, as working for the Lord, not for men. . . . It is the Lord Christ you are serving" (Colossians 3:23–24).

Priscilla's Legacy in Scripture

Read Acts 18:1–4.

1. Why did Priscilla and Aquila leave Rome and come to Corinth? What effect did this order of Claudius have on the spread of the gospel?

2. Paul had not only his faith but also his occupation in common with Priscilla and Aquila. Describe the special camaraderie you have with those who share your occupation and your faith.

Read Acts 18:18–19.

3. Priscilla and Aquila left Corinth and went with Paul to Ephesus. Would you be willing to move if God called you to do so to spread the truth of the gospel? Why or why not? Why would it be difficult or easy for you to make such a move?

Read Acts 18:20–21.

4. Priscilla and Aquila asked Paul to stay with them and "spend more time with them" in Ephesus. Perhaps they wished him to stay in order to learn more from him. But it is also possible that they were concerned for him and wished him to stay in order to give him the comfort of their home and companionship. Read 1 Corinthians 16:19 to find out what Priscilla and Aquila did in Paul's absence.

Read Acts 18:24–26.

5. Apollos needed further instruction in the truth, and Aquila and Priscilla took on the task. Note the way in which Priscilla and Aquila instructed him. What wisdom can you gain from Priscilla and Aquila's example of quietly taking Apollos aside to instruct him?

Read Romans 16:3–5.

6. It appears that Priscilla and Aquila are now back in Rome, moving from Rome to Corinth to Ephesus and back again. Priscilla moved a lot, but she obviously served wherever she lived. How can you apply her example to your life?

7. What does Paul here claim that Aquila and Priscilla did for him?

8. Have you ever risked your life for anyone? Have you ever experienced hardship in order to advance the cause of the gospel? Describe what happened.

9. What have you learned about Priscilla that helps you understand why Paul entrusted her and Aquila with leading a church in their home?

10. Note that every time Aquila and Priscilla's names appear, they appear together, sometimes one first, sometimes the other. What sort of couple does this make you think they were?

ALL THE WOMEN
OF THE BIBLE

Genesis

Eve	Ge 2–3; 2Co 11:3; 1Ti 2:13
Cain's Wife	Ge 4:17
Adah 1	Ge 4:19–23
Zillah	Ge 4:19–23
Naamah 1	Ge 4:22
Seth's Daughters	Ge 5:6–8
Enosh's Daughters	Ge 5:9–11
Kenan's Daughters	Ge 5:12–14
Mahalalel's Daughters	Ge 5:15–17
Jared's Daughters	Ge 5:18–20
Enoch's Daughters	Ge 5:21–24
Methuselah's Daughters	Ge 5:25–27
Lamech's Daughters	Ge 5:28–31
Daughters of Men	Ge 6:1–8
Noah's Wife/Son's Wives	Ge 6:18; 7:1, 7, 13; 8:16, 18
Shem's Daughters	Ge 11:11
Arphaxad's Daughters	Ge 11:13
Shelah's Daughters	Ge 11:15
Eber's Daughters	Ge 11:17
Peleg's Daughters	Ge 11:19
Reu's Daughters	Ge 11:21
Serug's Daughters	Ge 11:23
Nahor's Daughters	Ge 11:25
Sarah (Sarai)	Ge 11:29–31; 12:5–17; 16:1–8; 17:15–21; 18; 20:2–18; 21:1–12: 23:1–19; 24:36–37; 25:10, 12; 49:31; Isa 51:2; Ro 4:19; 9:9; Heb 11:11; 1Pe 3:6
Iscah	Ge 11:29
Milcah 1	Ge 11:29; 22:20, 23; 24:15, 24
Hagar	Ge 16; 21:9–17; 25:12; Gal 4:24–25

Lot's Daughters	Ge 19:12–17, 30–38
Lot's Wife	Ge 19:15–26; Lk 17:29–33
Rebekah	Ge 22:23; 24; 25:20–28; 26:6–35; 27; 28:5; 29:12; 35:8; 49:31; Ro 9:10–13
Deborah 1	Ge 24:59; 35:8
Keturah	Ge 25:1–6; 1Ch 1:32–33
Judith	Ge 26:34
Basemath 1	Ge 26:34; 36:3, 4, 10, 13, 17
Mahalath	Ge 28:9
Leah	Ge 29–30; 49:31; Ru 4:11
Rachel	Ge 29–31; 33:1–2, 7; 35:16–26; 46:19, 22, 25; 48:7; Ru 4:11; 1Sa 10:2; Jer 31:15; Mt 2:18
Zilpah	Ge 29:24; 30:9–10; 35:26; 37:2; 46:18
Bilhah	Ge 29:29; 30:2–7; 37:2; 46:25; 1Ch 7:13
Dinah	Ge 30:21; 34; 46:15
Oholibamah	Ge 36:2–25
Adah 2	Ge 36:2, 4, 10, 12, 16
Timna	Ge 36:12, 22; 1Ch 1:39
Matred	Ge 36:39; 1Ch 1:50
Mehetabel	Ge 36:39; 1Ch 1:50
Tamar 1	Ge 38:6–30; Ru 4:12; 1Ch 2:4; Mt 1:3
Potiphar's Wife	Ge 39
Asenath	Ge 41:45–50; 46:20
Shaul's Mother	Ge 46:10; Ex 6:15
Serah	Ge 46:17; 1Ch 7:30

Exodus

Puah	Ex 1:15
Shiphrah	Ex 1:15
Jochebed	Ex 2:1–10; 6:20; Nu 26:59; Heb 11:23

1 Kings

Abishag	1Ki 1–2
Two Prostitute Mothers	1Ki 3
Taphath	1Ki 4:11
Basemath 3	1Ki 4:15
Hiram's Mother	1Ki 7:13–45; 2Ch 2:13–14
Queen of Sheba	1Ki 10: 1–13; 2Ch 9:1–12; Mt 12:42
Solomon's Wives and Concubines	1Ki 11:1–18
Tahpenes	1Ki 11:19–20
Hadad's Wife	1Ki 11:19–20
Zeruah	1Ki 11:26–40
Jeroboam's Wife	1Ki 14:1–17
Naamah 2	1Ki 14:21, 31; 2Ch 12:13
Maacah 2	1Ki 15:1–2, 10, 13; 2Ch 11:20–22; 15:16
Jezebel 1	1Ki 16:31; 18:4–19; 19:1–2; 21:5–25; 2Ki 9
Widow of Zarephath	1Ki 17:8–24; Lk 4:25–26
Elisha's Mother	1Ki 19:20
Azubah 2	1Ki 22:42; 2Ch 20:31

2 Kings

Widow with Jars of Oil	2Ki 4:1–7
Woman of Shunem	2Ki 4:8–37; 8:1–6
Servant Girl of Naaman's Wife	2Ki 5:1–19
Naaman's Wife	2Ki 5:2–4
Mothers Who Ate Their Sons	2Ki 6:26–30
Athaliah	2Ki 8:26; 11; 2Ch 22; 23:13–21; 24:7
Jehosheba	2Ki 11:2; 2Ch 22:11
Zibiah	2Ki 12:1; 2Ch 24:1
Shimeath	2Ki 12:21; 2Ch 24:26
Shomer	2Ki 12:21
Jehoaddin	2Ki 14:2; 2Ch 25:1
Jerusha	2Ki 15:33; 2Ch 27:1
Jecoliah	2Ki 15:2; 2Ch 26:3
Abijah	2Ki 18:2; 2Ch 29:1
Hephzibah	2Ki 21:1; Isa 62:4
Meshullemeth	2Ki 21:19
Jedidah	2Ki 22:1–2
Huldah	2Ki 22:14–20; 2Ch 34:22–33
Hamutal	2Ki 23:31; 24:18; Jer 52:1–2
Zebidah	2Ki 23:36
Nehushta	2Ki 24:8; Jer 29:2

1 Chronicles

Jerioth	1Ch 2:18
Azubah 1	1Ch 2:18–19
Ephrath	1Ch 2:19, 50; 4:4
Abijah	1Ch 2:24
Atarah	1Ch 2:26
Abihail 2	1Ch 2:29
Ahlai 1	1Ch 2:31, 34
Sheshan's Daughters	1Ch 2:34–35
Ephah	1Ch 2:46
Maacah 3	1Ch 2:48
Shelomith 2	1Ch 3:19
Hazzelelponi	1Ch 4:3
Naarah	1Ch 4:5–6
Helah	1Ch 4:5, 7
Jabez's Mother	1Ch 4:9–10
Bithiah	1Ch 4:18
Hodiah's Wife	1Ch 4:19
Shimei's Daughters	1Ch 4:27
Maacah 4	1Ch 7:15–16
Hammoleketh	1Ch 7:18
Mahlah 1	1Ch 7:18
Sheerah	1Ch 7:24
Baara	1Ch 8:8
Hodesh	1Ch 8:9
Hushim	1Ch 8:8, 11 (see Nu 26:42; 1Ch 7:12)
Maacah 5	1Ch 8:29; 9:35
Heman's Daughters	1Ch 25:5–6

2 Chronicles

Abihail 3	2Ch 11:18
Mahalath	2Ch 11:18
Maacah 6	2Ch 13:2
Shimrith	2Ch 24:26

Ezra

Foreign Women	Ezr 9:2; 10:2–3, 18–19, 44

Nehemiah

Artaxerxes' Queen	Ne 2:6
Shallum's Daughters	Ne 3:12
Noadiah	Ne 6:14
Barzillai's Daughter	Ne 7:63–64
Women of Mixed Marriages	Ne 13:23–29

Esther

Vashti	Est 1; 2:1
Esther	Est 2–9
Zeresh	Est 5:10, 14; 6:13

Job

Job's Wife	Job 2:9–10
Jemimah	Job 42:14
Keziah	Job 42:14
Keren-Happuch	Job 42:14

Psalms

Daughters of Kings	Ps 45:9
Royal Bride	Ps 45:9–10
Virgin Companions	Ps 45:14
Barren Woman	Ps 113:9
Maid and Mistress	Ps 123:2

Proverbs

The Adulteress	Pr 2:16; 5:3–6
Wayward Wife	Pr 7
Lemuel's Mother	Pr 31:1
Wife of Noble Character	Pr 31

Ecclesiastes

Women Singers	Ecc 2:8
Deceitful Women	Ecc 7:26

Song of Songs

The Shulammite Woman	SS

Isaiah

Women of Zion	Isa 3:16–4:6
The Virgin	Isa 7:14–16
Isaiah's Wife	Isa 8:1–4
Complacent Women	Isa 32:9–20

Jeremiah

Queen of Heaven	Jer 7:18; 44:17–19
Jeremiah's Mother	Jer 15:10
Queen Mother	Jer 29:2
Zedekiah's Daughters	Jer 41:10
Wives Who Burned Incense	Jer 44:7–10, 15–30

Lamentations

Maidens	La 1:4, 18; 2:21
Young Women of Jerusalem	La 2:10
Mothers	La 2:12
Compassionate Women	La 4:10
Women and Virgins	La 5:11

Ezekiel

Women Who Mourned Tammuz	Eze 8:14
Daughters Who Prophesy	Eze 13:17–18
Oholah	Eze 23
Oholibah	Eze 23
Ezekiel's Wife	Eze 24:15–27

Daniel

Belteshazzar's Queen	Da 5:10–12
Daughter of the King of the South	Da 11:6–9, 17

Hosea

Gomer	Hos 1:1–11; 3:1–5
Lo-Ruhamah	Hos 1:6, 8

Joel

A Virgin	Joel 1:8
A Bride	Joel 2:16
Spirit-Filled Women	Joel 2:29
Girls	Joel 3:3

Amos

Oppressive Women	Am 4:1
Daughters	Am 7:17
Young Women	Am 8:13

Obadiah

Jonah

Micah

Women of My People	Mic 2:9
Daughter	Mic 7:6
Mother	Mic 7:6
Daughter-in-Law	Mic 7:6
Mother-in-Law	Mic 7:6

Nahum

Harlot	Na 3:4

Habakkuk

Zephaniah

Haggai

Zechariah

Woman in a Basket	Zec 5:7
Old Women	Zec 8:4
Girls	Zec 8:5
Young Women	Zec 9:17

Malachi

Daughter of a Foreign God	Mal 2:11
The Wife of Their Youth	Mal 2:14–15

Matthew

Mary, Mother of Jesus	Mt 1–2; 12; 12:46; Mk 3:31–35; Lk 1:39–56; 8:19–21; Jn 2:1–5; 19:25; Ac 1:14
Peter's Mother-in-Law	Mt 8:14–18; Mk 1:29–34; Lk 4:38–41
Woman with the Issue of Blood	Mt 9:20–22; Mk 5:25–34; Lk 8:43–48
Jairus's Daughter	Mt 9:18–25; Mk 5:21–43; Lk 8:41–56
Woman and Her Dough	Mt 13:33; Lk 13:21
Jesus' Sisters	Mt 13:55–56; Mk 6:3
Herodias	Mt 14:3–12; Mk 6:14–24; Lk 3:19–20
Salome 1 (Daughter of Herodias)	Mt 14:6–11: Mk 6:22–28
Syrophoenician Woman	Mt 15:21–28; Mk 7:24–30
Wife Sold for Debt	Mt 18:25
Mother of the Zebedees (Salome)	Mt 20:20–24; 27:56; Mk 15:40–41; 16:1–2
Woman with Seven Husbands	Mt 22:25–32; Lk 20:27–38
Women at the Mill	Mt 24:41
Ten Virgins	Mt 25:1–7
Servant Girls at Peter's Denial	Mt 26:69–71; Mk 14:66–69; Lk 22:56–59; Jn 18:16–17

Pilate's Wife	Mt 27:19
Women at Calvary	Mt 27:55
Mary Magdalene	Mt 27:56, 61; 28:1; Mk 15:40–41, 47; 16:1–19; Lk 8:2; 24:10; Jn 19:25; 20:1–18
Mary, Mother of James and Joses	Mt 27:56, 61; 28:1; Mk 15:40–41, 47; 16:1; Lk 24:10; Jn 19:25

Mark

Widow with Two Mites	Mk 12:41–44; Lk 21:1–4

Luke

Elizabeth	Lk 1:5–80
Anna	Lk 2:36–38
Widow of Nain	Lk 7:11–18
Sinful Woman at Simon's House	Lk 7:36–50
Joanna	Lk 8:1–3; 23:55; 24:10
Susanna	Lk 8:2–3
Mary of Bethany	Lk 10:38–41; Jn 11; 12:1–3
Martha	Lk 10:38–41; Jn 11; 12:1–3
A Woman in the Crowd	Lk 11:27–28
Crippled Woman	Lk 13:11–13
Woman Who Lost the Silver Coin	Lk 15:8–10
Importunate Widow	Lk 18:1–8
Daughters of Jerusalem	Lk 23:28–30

John

Woman at the Well	Jn 4
Woman Caught in Adultery	Jn 8:1–11
Woman Giving Birth	Jn 16:20–21

Acts

Sapphira	Ac 5:1–11
Jewish Widows	Ac 6:1–4
Candace	Ac 8:27
Dorcas (Tabitha)	Ac 9:36–43
Mary (Mother of John Mark)	Ac 12
Rhoda	Ac 12:1–19
Women of Antioch	Ac 13:50
Timothy's Mother	Ac 16:1
Lydia	Ac 16:12–15, 40

TIMELINE OF WOMEN OF THE BIBLE

B.C.	2000	1500	1000	500	1 A.D.	500

Eve

Noah's Wife

Sarah

Lot's Wife

Hagar

Rebekah

Leah

Rachel

Moses' Mothers

Miriam

Rahab

Deborah (1225)

Hannah

Samson's Mother

Delilah

Naomi

Ruth

Michal

Abigail

Bathsheba

Queen of Sheba

Jezebel

Widow of Zarephath

Athaliah

Woman of Shunem

Gomer

Vashti

Esther

Anna

Elizabeth

Mary

Mary Magdalene

Mary of Bethany

Martha

Woman at the Well

Adulterous Woman

Sapphira

Dorcas

Rhoda

Lydia

Priscilla

Lois

Eunice

SONS OF JACOB

MOTHER	SON	MEANING OF NAME	REFERENCE OF BIRTH (GENESIS)	ORDER OF BLESSING	SYMBOL OF BLESSING	REFERENCE OF BLESSING (GENESIS)
L E A H	Reuben	Behold, a son	29:32	1	Reckless	49:3–4
	Simeon	Hearing	29:33	2	Violence	49:5–7
	Levi	Attachment	29:34	3	Violence	49:5–7
	Judah	Praise	29:35	4	Lion	49:8–12
B I L H A H	Dan	Judgment	30:6	7	Serpent	49:16–18
	Naphtali	Wrestle	30:8	10	Doe	49:21
Z I L P A H	Gad	Good fortune	30:11	8	Raider	49:19
	Asher	Happy	30:13	9	Rich food	49:20
L E A H	Issachar	Reward	30:18	6	Donkey	49:14–15
	Zebulun	Abode	30:20	5	Ships	49:13
R A C H E L	Joseph	May he add	30:24	11	Fruitful	49:22–26
	Benjamin	Son of the right hand	35:18	12	Wolf	49:27

JEWISH CALENDAR

Reli-gious Year	Civil Year	Hebrew Month	Western Correlation	Farm Seasons	Clim-ate	Special Days
1	7	Nisan	March–April	Barley harvest	Latter Rains (Mal-qosh)	14—Passover 21—Firstfruits
2	8	Iyyar	April–May	General harvest		
3	9	Sivan	May–June	Wheat harvest Vine tending	D R Y S E A S O N	6—Pentecost
4	10	Tammuz	June–July	First grapes		
5	11	Ab	July–August	Grapes, figs, olives		9—Destruction of Temple
6	12	Elul	August–September	Vintage		
7	1	Tishri	September–October	Plowing		1—New Year 10—Day of Atonement 15-21—Feast of Tabernacles
8	2	Marchesvan	October–November	Grain planting		
9	3	Kislev	November–December		Early Rains (Yoreh)	25—Dedication
10	4	Tebet	December–January	Spring growth		
11	5	Shebat	January–February	Winter figs	Rain Season	
12	6	Adar	February–March	Pulling flax Almonds bloom		13-14—Purim
		Adar Sheni	Intercalary Month			

WOMEN IN JESUS' FAMILY TREE

Abraham (Sarah)
Isaac (Rebekah)
Jacob (Leah)
Judah (Tamar)
Perez (unknown)
Hezron (unknown)
Ram (unknown)
Amminadab (unknown)
Nahshon (unknown)
Salmon (Rahab)
Boaz (Ruth)
Obed (unknown)
Jesse (unknown)
David (Bathsheba)
Solomon (Naamah)
Rehoboam (Maacah)
Abijah (unknown)
Asa (Azubah)
Jehoshaphat (unknown)
Jehoram (Athaliah)
Uzziah (Jerusha)
Jotham (unknown)
Ahaz (Abijah)
Hezekiah (Hephzibah)
Manasseh (unknown)
Amon (Jedidah)
Josiah (Zebidah)
Jehoiachin (unknown)
Shealtiel (unknown)
Zerubbabel (unknown)
Abiud (unknown)
Eliakim (unknown)
Azor (unknown)
Zadok (unknown)
Akim (unknown)
Eliud (unknown)
Eleazar (unknown)
Matthan (unknown)
Jacob (unknown)
Joseph (Mary)

JESUS

WOMEN IN JESUS' LIFE AND MINISTRY

Jesus Meets ...	What Happens	Scripture
Mary, his mother	She loves him as her son and Savior.	Mt 1–2; 12:46–50 Mk 3:31–35 Lk 1–2; 8:19–21 Jn 2:1–11; 19:25 Ac 1:14
Elizabeth	She gives birth to Jesus' forerunner.	Lk 1:5–80
Anna	She praises God for the baby Jesus.	Lk 2:36–38
Woman at the well	She believes Jesus is the Messiah.	Jn 4:1–42
Peter's mother-in-law	Jesus heals her.	Mt 8:14–15 Mk 1:29–31 Lk 4:38–39
Widow of Nain	Jesus raises her son from the dead.	Lk 7:11–17
Sinful woman at Simon's house	She washes Jesus' feet with her tears.	Lk 7:36–50
Joanna	She supports Jesus financially.	Lk 8:1–3; 23:55; 24:10
Susanna	She helps Jesus in his ministry.	Lk 8:1–3
Woman with the issue of blood	She is healed when she touches Jesus.	Mt 9:20–22 Mk 5:25–34 Lk 8:43–48
Jairus's daughter	Jesus raises her from death.	Mt 9:18–26 Mk 5:21–43 Lk 8:41–56
Syrophoenician woman	Jesus responds to her plea.	Mt 15:21–28 Mk 7:24–30
Woman caught in adultery	Jesus saves her and tells her to sin no more.	Jn 8:1–11
Mary of Bethany	She sits at Jesus' feet.	Lk 10:38–42 Jn 11; 12:1–8
Martha	Jesus sets her priorities straight.	Lk 10:38–42 Jn 11:12:1–2
A woman in the crowd	She calls out a blessing on Jesus' mother.	Lk 11:27–28
Crippled woman	Jesus heals her.	Lk 13:10–13
Mother of James and John	She asks Jesus a favor, and he admonishes her.	Mt 20:20–28; 27:56 Mk 15:40–41; 16:1–2
Widow with two coins	She models a lesson on giving for the disciples.	Mk 12:41–44 Lk 21:1–4
Daughters of Jerusalem	They weep as Jesus walks to his death.	Lk 23:27–31
Women at Calvary	They mourn as Jesus dies.	Mt 27:55
Mary, the mother of James and Joses	She helps take care of Jesus.	Mt 27:56, 61; 28:1 Mk 15:40–41, 47; 16:1 Lk 24:10; Jn 19:25
Mary Magdalene	She faithfully follows Jesus.	Mt 27:56, 61; 28:1 Mk 15:40–47; 16:1–11 Lk 8:1–10; 24:10 Jn 19:25; 20:1–18

MONEY

COINAGE	SYSTEM EQUIVALENT	U.S. EQUIVALENT[1]	KJV	NIV	NASB	SCRIPTURE EXAMPLE
Greek: drachma (*drachmē*)	day's wage	$.16	pieces of silver	silver coins	silver coins	Luke 15:8
two drachmas (*didrachmon*)	2 days' wages	$.32	tribute	two drachmas	two drachmas	Matthew 17:24
four drachmas (*statēr*)	4 days' wages	$.64	piece of money	four drachmas	stater	Matthew 17:27
Roman: denarius (*dēnarion*)	day's wage	$.20	pence penny	denarius silver coins day's wage	denarii denarii denarius	Matthew 18:28 Luke 10:35 Revelation 6:6
assarion	1/16 of a denarius or of a drachma	c. $.01	farthing	penny	cent	Matthew 10:29
kodrantes	1/64 of a denarius or of a drachma	c. 1/4 of $.01	farthing	penny	cent	Matthew 5:26
lepton (Jewish?)	1/128 of a denarius or of a drachma	1/8 of $.01	mite	very small copper coins	small copper coins	Mark 12:42
argyrion (silver)	day's wage shekel, 4 drachmas or Attic silver, 1 drachma	$.16	pieces of silver	penny silver coins drachma	cent pieces of silver pieces of silver	Luke 12:59 Matthew 26:15 Acts 19:19
chrysos (gold)	aureus (Roman coin) 25 denarii	$5.00	gold	gold	gold	Matthew 10:19
talanton	240 aurei (value of one silver talent)	$1,200.00[2]	talents	talents	talents	Matthew 18:24
mina (*mna*)	1/60 of a talent	$20.00[2]	pounds	mina	minas	Luke 19:13–25

[1] Since inflation continually changes the equivalent of U.S. value, the current rate of exchange with the first century has been used rather than (let's say) the current minimum wage, e.g., 1981, $3.35 = $26.80. For the current earning power equivalent, one need only use a computation as given before in view of minimum wage in force.

[2] Talent and mina also refer to weight. When monetary amount is intended, the value depends on whether the coins are silver or gold. *Chrysos* is the Greek word for gold, not for a specific coins; but in Matthew 10:9 it probably refers to money, either to the Roman *aureus* mentioned above, or to the half *aureus*, which Rome also circulated.

THE REIGNS OF THE HERODS

Name	Dates of Reign	Title	Territory	NT Period
Herod the Great	37-4 B.C.	King	Judea, Samaria, Galilee, Perea, Idumea, Traconitis	time of Jesus' birth
Herod Philip II	4 B.C.-A.D. 34	Tetrarch	Iturea, Traconitis	Jesus' infancy till after his death and resurrection
Herod Antipas	4 B.C.-A.D. 39	Tetrarch	Galilee and Perea	Jesus' infancy till after his death and resurrection
Herod Archelaus	4 B.C.-A.D. 6	Ethnarch	Judea, Idumea, Samaria	Jesus' infancy till his early childhood
Herod Agrippa I	A.D. 37-44	King	Judea, Samaria, Galilee, Perea, Idumea, northeast Palestine	early years after Pentecost
Herod Agrippa II	A.D. 50-70	Tetrarch	Tiberias, Batanea, Traconitis, Auranitis, Abila	during the spread of Christianity to the Gentiles

THE HEROD FAMILY IN THE NEW TESTAMENT

(Note: Names appearing in bold type are those family members who are mentioned in the NT.)

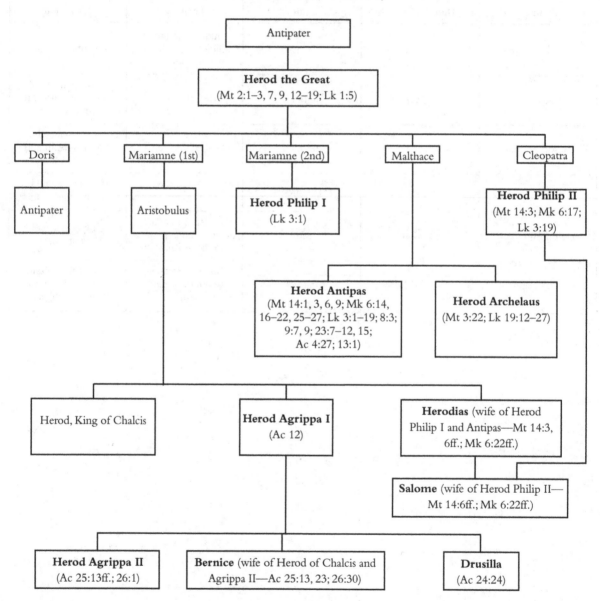

Praying the Names of God

Ann Spangler

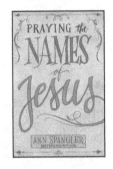

Praying the Names of Jesus

Ann Spangler

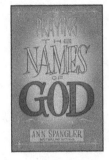

Names in the ancient world did more than simply distinguish one person from another; they often conveyed the essential nature and character of a person. This is especially true when it comes to the names of God recorded in the Bible. *Praying the Names of God* explores the primary names and titles of God in the Old Testament to reveal the deeper meanings behind them. *Praying the Names of Jesus* does the same thing for Jesus in the New Testament.

By understanding the biblical context in which these names and titles are revealed, readers gain a more intimate knowledge of Jesus and of his plan for their lives.

Available in stores and online!

ZONDERVAN
.com